A
Social H of

BODMIN UNION WORKHOUSE

by

Tony Philp

Published by
Bodmin Town Museum,
Mount Folly, Bodmin, Cornwall, PL31 2HQ

About the Author

Tony Philp is a graduate with a degree in geography who has spent his working life in local government in the field of town planning. Now retired he lived at Castle Hill Court for 11 years between 1989 and 2000. He set up a Residents Association, with a small Committee of owners to take responsibility for managing the 35 flat complex. Having always had an interest in local affairs he researched the history of the workhouse over the period of 11 years during which he lived there. This book is the culmination of a more intensive period of work since his retirement in 1998, and was completed by the end of 2000.

ISBN 0-9549913-0-3

Printed by MPG Books Ltd, Bodmin, Cornwall

Contents

Dedication

To My Friends at Castle Hill Court

This book has been written as a contribution to the record of the social history of Bodmin. It endeavours to convey the conditions experienced by those less fortunate beings who crossed the workhouse threshold, and the efforts made by the paid officials and elected members to relieve the burdens of poverty. The individuals concerned have passed on, but the buildings remain, still with an ambience generated by the workhouse era. Strangely, an ambience now of peace and quiet, shared by all those who live there in a recycled phase when once again the buildings are providing refuge and shelter.

December, 2000

Sources of Information

The workhouse system was nothing if not bureaucratic. One of the main tasks of the Master of the local workhouse was record-keeping, and all of the meetings of the locally elected Guardians had to be meticulously minuted. During the nineteenth century central government issued and enforced the regulations so that a constant interchange of correspondence and visits occurred between the local workhouse and London.

Sources of information would therefore appear likely to be plentiful; but, alas, this is not the case in reality. The majority of records for most workhouses, including Bodmin, have with time become dissipated in various directions, and ultimately lost.

In writing this book I have found two sources of surviving information to be the most fruitful - the records of the national poor law authorities, and local newspaper reports.

The records of the national poor law authorities are in the Public Record Office at Kew. Class MH 12 contains the volumes of correspondence relating to the operation of the poor law in each local union for the period 1834-1900. Most of the correspondence for the period after 1900 was destroyed by bombing during the Second World War. MH/12/1274-1295 are the 21 volumes of correspondence relating to the Bodmin Union, and where items of information have been extracted for this book they are referenced to the appropriate volume in the text.

A separate source of information at the Public Record Office is the Register of Workhouse Officers for the period 1837-1921. This contains the full names of all the paid local officials, the dates of their service, details of their payments, and the reasons for resignation. MH/9/3 is the volume containing the Bodmin Union details, and material extracted from it is acknowledged at appropriate points in the text.

The Cornish Guardian is the local newspaper covering the Bodmin area and was first published in January, 1901. The fortnightly meetings of the Board of Guardians are regularly reported from that date, along with other occasional features and reports relating to life in the Bodmin Union workhouse. The County library in Bodmin holds a complete microfilm copy of the Cornish Guardian editions and where newspaper reports have been used in the text they are referenced with the prefix CG, followed by the date of the relevant edition. By coincidence these reports have filled the gap which would have otherwise occurred with the loss of the national records.

The formal minute books recording the local Board of Guardian meetings for the period 1842-1916, such as have survived, are held in the County Record Office at Truro. They were found to be of more limited value than the national records but where information has been extracted it is acknowledged in the text by reference to the appropriate volume in the run of 11 volumes PU/BOD/1-11. A further separate volume from which ancillary staffing information has been extracted is PU/BOD/39, the Officers' Salaries Register, 1878-1929.

Prior to 1901 useful newspaper reports were not found, but advertisements relating to the building of the workhouse, the recruitment of staff, and the procurement of supplies do appear in the Royal Cornwall Gazette. Microfilm copies of this newspaper from 1801 are held in the Cornish Studies library at Redruth. Copies of these interesting advertisements are included in the text. Copies of photographs which appeared originally in the Cornish Guardian newspaper have also been included in the text.

The decennial Census enumerator's books for 1841-1901 provide an invaluable insight into who was living in the Bodmin Union workhouse on the night of each census. They record the names and personal details of the workhouse officers, and the details of the inmates. Microfilm copies were read at the Cornish Studies library, Redruth, and paper copies of a computer database for 1851 and 1881 were obtained from the Courtney library, the Royal Institution of Cornwall, Truro.

The detailed plans of the original workhouse have been lost. However, the 1880 First Edition Ordnance Survey maps provide interesting clues in attempting to unravel the various functions and uses of the different buildings on the workhouse site. Extracts of these maps are incorporated into the text, together with various photographs of the workhouse buildings both pre and post their conversions at the end of the 1980s.

This book has been written with the benefit of information extracted from various other publications and sources. These are each referenced in the text, and full details are given at the end of the book.

To conclude this section on sources of information, I would like to record my gratitude and thanks to the staff at each record office and library which I have visited for their time and patience in assisting me with my researches; to local people who have made helpful contributions; and, finally, to the local Bodmin Town Museum for enabling publication some 5 years after completion.

Chapter 1

Introduction

The workhouse, synonymous for many people with the tale of Oliver Twist by Charles Dickens, was one of the social innovations of the Victorian age. In the mid 1800s hundreds of workhouses were erected across the country, at roughly 20 mile intervals, accompanied by major changes in the social administration associated with the poor. In many ways the workhouse system was the forerunner of the specialised caring institutions of the 20th century. But, it created a number of myths, rather than achieving its original aims.

The new social administration which gave rise to the workhouse introduced the concept of a system of local government looking beyond the boundaries of the individual parish, the unit of public affairs since Elizabethan times. Parishes were required to combine together into larger Unions, each with their own workhouse, workhouse officials, and elected representatives to administer it. The concept has been modified since with successive local government re-organisations, but it can claim to be the origin of modern local administration, particularly in the extensive rural areas of the country, outside the towns and cities with their much older corporations.

Workhouses themselves provided services for their inmates which outside had yet to become available for the masses of the working class. Workhouse infirmaries were ahead of the outside voluntary hospitals and provided some form of care for the sick in many parts of the country where no other service was available; workhouse schools offered a basic education for pauper children, long before the problem of illiteracy in the masses was addressed by the provision outside of free education for all; workhouses in general offered an asylum to dependent people who were unfortunate enough to have no other recourse.

On the other hand, despite being apparently ahead of its time, the workhouse never tackled successfully the main type of inmate for whom it was specifically designed - the able bodied poor, living on parish hand outs, and evading the chances of employment necessary to become self sufficient. Many such persons either remained outside the system altogether and survived by begging or stealing, or dipped into the system, with varying degrees of manipulation, but managed to achieve the main aim of staying outside the workhouse itself. Instead of instilling the Victorian work ethic in the poor, and eliminating poverty, the workhouse in many Unions was filled with the young unmarried mother with her bastard child or children; orphaned or abandoned children; the feeble minded; and the old and infirm without any relatives able or willing to care for them.

Whilst direct success in converting the poor to work and reducing the financial burden on the state eluded the workhouse system, it can claim a significant success on a psychological level. The vast majority of the working class masses feared the possibility of incarceration in the workhouse more than anything else, for various reasons - the sense of shame; the sense of failure; and the tales, often untrue and exaggerated, of the cruel regime within. Working class children were regularly reminded by parents with the threat of the local workhouse if they shirked to "make the grade", and such memories remain with people today. The number who, under this fear or threat, avoided the stigma of the workhouse can never be counted, but it was the deterrent effect which was the measure of the success of the workhouse system.

Many of the original workhouse buildings remain today, in various uses and having been altered through conversions to varying degrees. Few though appear to have had their own stories recorded in any detail, an unfortunate omission for future generations. They are merely given scant mention in a local history or a more general history of the poor. This account attempts to fill that gap, however imperfectly due mainly to the paucity of records which have survived, for the Bodmin Union workhouse.

Chapter 2

The National Context

The history of Bodmin Union workhouse is inextricably bound up with the national scene as it unfolded during the 19th century for dealing with the poor.

From the 16th century to the beginning of the 19th century it was the ecclesiastical parish which was responsible, through the elected members of the Parish Council or Vestry, for the care of the poor and sick, for the maintenance of parish roads, and for the levying of rates to finance this expenditure. In the case of the poor, most parish relief was granted in the form of "out relief". This comprised the payment of money and/or provision of food, clothing, and other goods to paupers who continued to live in their own cottages or relatives' homes *(Herber, M.D.)*. The amount of relief given was determined according to the varying price of bread and the size of the family. Sometimes the able bodied were required to undertake communal work for the parish, but this was not always the case.

A second form of parish relief in some parishes was the "indoor relief" in the local poorhouse. These early workhouses originated in the 18th century, and were principally intended for the sick, elderly, and orphans *(Herber, M.D.)*. In 1756 a parish poor house was erected in Bodmin as the town's first purpose built workhouse, on the site of the recently closed Post Office at the bottom of Crinnick's Hill. It was erected, at the expense of Sir William Irby, Bt, then one of the Borough's two representatives in Parliament, on land given by the Borough Council or Corporation *(Long, L.E.)*. Its supervision would have been the responsibility of the churchwardens and the parish overseer, the latter being the most important official who implemented day to day duties under the Poor Law Act of 1601.

By the early 19th century these systems of poor relief became increasingly expensive and ineffective. By 1834, mostly due to the recent rapid rise in population at that time, the cost of poor relief for the whole country had risen to £6.3M, an average expenditure of 10s per head of population *(Longmate, N.)*. Furthermore, it encouraged people to avoid work and to live on parish relief, as well as allowing employers to pay low wages as the parish would ensure workers and their families did not starve *(Herber, M.D.)*.

In February 1832 the Poor Law Commission was appointed by Parliament and began working on "...a diligent and full inquiry into the practical operation of the Laws for the Relief of the Poor in England and Wales, and into the manner in which those laws are administered..." Between 1832 and 1834, 9 Commissioners, headed by Edwin Chadwick, investigated conditions amongst the poor of England and Wales. Questionnaires were sent to 3000 Poor Law Authorities, one fifth of the total number. In 1834 the English Poor Law Report was produced, and has been described as "...one of the classical documents of western social history"...(Checkland, S.G. & Checkland, E.O.A.).

Based on the findings of the Commissioners Report, the 1834 Poor Law Amendment Act came into effect, one of the most controversial and influential pieces of legislation of the century.

Two main principles in the new Act changed relief for the poor as previously administered - "the workhouse test" and "less eligibility".

"The workhouse test" was based on the abolition of "outdoor relief" for all able bodied people seeking relief, unless they entered the workhouse. Whilst the aged or infirm could still obtain "outdoor relief" outside the workhouse, it was hoped that for the able bodied the new system would soon bring the work shy to heel. If the sick poor had to be accommodated in the workhouse, either because they could not be cared for at home, or because they fell ill whilst in the workhouse, it was recommended that they should be housed apart from the able bodied, and have a less severe routine.

The other deterrent arm of the Act, "less eligibility", was defined in the Poor Law Report as "...the restoration of the pauper to a position below that of the independent labourer..". The intention was to make "indoor relief" in the workhouse as unattractive as possible in order to deter all but the destitute, the only genuine applicant for relief.

Efficiency and discipline were to be the important new features of poor relief with the 1834 Act. The Act removed control from individual parishes and intended that a centrally directed, uniform system for Unions of parishes would be developed across the entire country.

The implementation of the 1834 Act was achieved through three levels of administration. At the centre in London were the three permanent Central Commissioners, with secretary, Edwin Chadwick, intent on organising, legislating, and directing the working of the Act overall. Assistant Commissioners were appointed to be responsible for different parts of the country. Their main duties were to supervise the formation of the Unions, and to ensure that adequate arrangements were provided according to the plethora of regulations. At the local level individual parishes were grouped together to form a Union, whose activities were prescribed by regulation, and closely monitored by the central authority. By 1838, 573 Unions had been constituted across England from 13000 parishes *(May, T.)*.

Once a Union had been formed and declared, the chief priority was to persuade the members of the Union, referred to as the Guardians, to build a new workhouse. Few of the previous poorhouses were adequate in size, or met the strict requirements of the new legislation. The first Annual Report of the Poor Law Commissioners in 1835 included an appendix containing a number of model plans for workhouses on which Unions had to base their own buildings. Deviations from model plans were acceptable to meet local conditions, but there was a safeguard that all plans had to be submitted by the Boards of local Unions for approval by Commissioners as regards design and cost. Sites for workhouses had to be chosen carefully so that they were reasonably central to the Union for paupers to walk to it from surrounding parishes, whilst at the same time attempting to allow them no nearer than the very periphery of towns. On prominent, readily visible sites, the deterrent effect to the working classes of the local "bastille" or "union house", as workhouses became known, was a constant reminder. In practice Union workhouses were erected at distances of roughly 20 miles (32kms) from each other. In the period 1834-39 some 350 were constructed, mostly in the more agricultural and south of the country. By 1883 a total of 554 new workhouses had been built *(May, T.)*.

To operate the workhouse system three groups of people were involved - the Poor Law Commissioners, the Union Guardians, and the salaried Union officials. Central regulations and accountability to the Commissioners dominated the system in the early years *(Crowther, M.A.)*. The priority concerns were:

* Enforced separation between different ages and sexes;
* Provision of a school for children;
* Setting the able bodied to work and giving them plain, frugal, but sufficient, food;
* Banning of tobacco and alcohol;
* Separate wards for the sick;
* Enforcement of cleanliness, order, and ventilation to ensure hygiene and discipline;
* Removal of all clothes and personal effects from the pauper on entry, and retaining them until his/her departure;
* Wearing of standard issue workhouse clothes;
* Detention within the workhouse at all times and no venturing outside without permission;

* The right for a pauper to discharge him/herself at will, having given a day's notice;
* Elaborate rules for punishment for paupers who committed workhouse offences.

The Assistant Commissioners initially between 1834-1847, then the Poor Law Inspectors when the Poor Law Commission was retitled the Poor Law Board between 1847-1871, and finally the General Inspectors when the Poor Law Board passed on to the Local Government Board between 1871-1919, were the linchpins between the central policy body of the Government, and the local Unions, where the policies and their detailed regulations were intended to be followed uniformly throughout the land. In reality, conditions varied significantly from workhouse to workhouse, and from Union Board to Union Board *(Crowther, M.A.)*. Inspectors visited every workhouse at least once during every year, and in some cases 2-3 times a year *(Preston-Thomas, H.)*. Their reports give vivid descriptions of conditions over the years. They met with Union Boards to discuss their findings and to stress improvements and changes which were necessary to comply with current regulations. Workhouse schools and teachers were inspected regularly, and all workhouse supplies and accounts were subject to regular, minute scrutiny by central government auditors.

At the local Union level it was the Guardians representing each parish within the Union who made the detailed local decisions affecting those seeking poor relief. Applications from paupers seeking relief were determined by them, and the detailed administration of the workhouse had to be regularly reported on and agreed by them. Their decisions determined the directions that the lives of many paupers took after they had fallen to needing the help of the Union purse.

Initially, after the introduction of the 1834 Act many Guardians were appointed by the former Parish Vestries, before their replacement by the new Union Boards for the administration of poor relief. Justices of the Peace were ex officio members of the new Boards. Election of Guardians by the ratepayers, rather than appointment, came gradually, but it made little difference to the type of Guardian, as few people possessed the necessary property qualifications to either put their names forward to stand for election, or to be able to vote at that time. When elections were necessary they were often not contested and the same people, virtually self appointed, tended to remain in office year after year *(Longmate, N.)*. This was particularly the case in the rural areas and was a distinct factor in changes being resisted longer than elsewhere. It was mainly the middle classes, clergy, doctors, lawyers, traders, farmers, and other professionals, who took on the job of being a Guardian for most of the 19th century.

It was not until the 1890s, and in particular the changes in the law introduced in 1894, that there was any fundamental changes in the composition of Guardians and Union Boards. At that time the property owning qualification for standing as a Guardian was abolished, so that anyone who had lived in a Union for a year could stand for election; and anyone enjoying parliamentary franchise, almost all males over the age of 21 years, acquired the right to vote *(Longmate,N.)*. These changes produced a greater interest in the post of Guardian, working class Guardians displaced some of the established "old brigade" on the Board, and women Guardians became more numerous. Combined with increasing changes in the central regulations giving far greater local discretion to Union Boards for their own affairs, the role of the Guardian in affecting the life of the pauper became greater.

There is no doubt that, whilst many Guardians performed their duties with a sense of compassion and desire to improve the lot of the pauper, the sense of local importance and power over the lives of less fortunate beings was never far from the minds of many Board members. There was always a degree of impasse with the central authority, whether the Poor Law Commission, the Poor Law Board, or the Local Government Board. Local Guardians resented having to implement central regulations *(May, T.)*. In many instances they refused to do so, or dragged their feet as long as possible to avoid making changes until the criticism of the central Inspector on his visits could no longer be resisted. The overriding desire to keep the local poor law tax as low as possible was another excuse for avoiding expenditure, and resisting improvements to the workhouse which would have made the inmates more comfortable *(May,T.)*. The parsimonious attitude of Guardians and Boards extended to the salaries and conditions of workhouse staff. Differing salaries offered by different Unions resulted in the movement of staff between workhouses, and the subject of remuneration was often a cause of strain between Guardians and their staff *(Crowther, M.A.)*.

The local Union Board met regularly every fortnight in the Board Room at the workhouse to conduct its business. The Board was required to be advised by a salaried official, properly qualified and versed in the Poor Law regulations. The Clerk to the Board was normally a local solicitor, who would endeavour to ensure that the actions of the Guardians were within the law. Once again tensions, to varying degrees, arose at times with the Clerk when Board Members totally disagreed with a central mandate and wanted to go their own way.

Also attending Board meetings, and appointed by local Guardians, were the

Relieving Officers. They had the responsibility for the distribution of financial relief, "outrelief", to the majority of the poor who had sought it and continued to live outside the confines of the workhouse. Whilst indoor paupers in the workhouse remained at the level nationally of 7.7/1000 head of population between 1849 and 1908, outdoor paupers still remained well above this level at 15.4/1000 in 1908, having fallen from 54.4/1000 in 1849 *(Preston-Thomas, H.)*. In the course of their duties there would inevitably be cases reported on by the Relieving Officers, and decided by the Guardians, where rather than continuing with further financial relief, a poor family would be relieved of one or more of their children who would be removed from the family to the workhouse and maintained there at public expense.

As far as workhouse officials were concerned, the 1834 Act intended that all Unions would employ a master and matron, a porter, a schoolteacher, a medical officer, and a chaplain *(Crowther, M.A.)*. In most Unions the problem was attracting and retaining quality staff. Posts in the workhouse were viewed as inferior to equivalent professional posts at that time outside. Pay and conditions were in most cases poor, and compared badly with other public services, most notably the prison service. Officials were all under the control of the master, and had to reside in the workhouse at all times, leaving to go into the outside world only with the master's permission. In many ways they ended up more incarcerated and institutionalised than the inmates, who at least could escape at a day's notice.

The main function of the master was to instill discipline in the workhouse. He was to "...enforce industry, order, punctuality, and cleanliness...", to see that the able bodied were put to work, to call the medical officer in case of illness, and to keep accounts of workhouse stores and property *(Crowther, M.A.)*.

It was essential for any aspirant master that he had a wife, who on his appointment would then become the matron of the workhouse. Her duties were to take care of the female paupers, concern herself with the nursing of the sick, and to manage the domestic work of the house *(Crowther, M.A.)*.

The porter's position was the humblest, but at the same time the most onerous. He was expected to command the respect of all the inmates, prevent unauthorised entry to the workhouse, admit all who applied for poor relief, and search all entering for forbidden commodities such as tobacco or alcohol *(Crowther, M.A.)*.

The workhouse doctor, or Medical Officer, was regarded as second rate in the medical profession. Nearly all combined their workhouse duties with private practice, and they only accepted underpaid workhouse posts because they couldn't support themselves adequately with their other work. The doctor had to refer to the master and often his recommendations were overruled. In treating the sick he had to provide all drugs and medical appliances out of his own salary, but extra fees could be claimed for smallpox vaccinations, midwifery, and certain surgical operations. His other duties included advising on possible health hazards in the workhouse, and advising the master on the classification of paupers for diet and work purposes. Until the links between disease, public health, and personal hygiene were established, fever epidemics were rife in workhouses and their infirmaries. Most nursing was done for many years by the paupers themselves, under the supervision of the matron. Paid nursing staff with any degree of training did not start to appear until towards the end of the 19th century. It was the increasing gap between the standards in the outside voluntary hospitals, compared to those in the workhouse infirmaries, which gradually led to improving reforms *(Crowther, M.A.)*.

Workhouse schoolteachers varied enormously in ability. Initially, many were unqualified and any literate person could apply for the post. Later, teachers were subjected to annual inspection and testing which determined their salary grading as well as helping to raise standards. Workhouse school lessons, however, remained basic, and attempted to instil some degree of literacy and numeracy in workhouse children. Alongside teaching, schoolteachers also had to supervise the children constantly, often having to bathe them, mend their clothes and act as general nurse *(Crowther, M.A.)*.

The post of chaplain in the workhouse was even more tenuous and some Unions never appointed one. Workhouse regulations required grace to be said at all meals, which was performed by the master, and religious services, such as they were, were performed by visiting clergy from local churches *(Crowther, M.A.)*.

With the passage of time through the 19th century the iron grip of central control, as intended in the 1834 Act and its regulations, gradually lessened, particularly as reformers exposed the inhumanities of the workhouse system. Changes came, in particular during and after the 1870s when the Poor Law Commission became the Local Government Board.

In 1880 school attendance by all children became obligatory, and the opening of local board schools outside the workhouse for local children provided far better standards than most workhouse schools. Cost savings on workhouse teachers, and a recognition that workhouse children could benefit from going outside the confines of the workhouse to local schools, led to the demise of workhouse schools by the end of the century *(Crowther, M.A.)*. Accompanying this was the abolition of distinctive workhouse clothes so that pauper children were no longer picked out in the school playground.

Changes in the election of Guardians during the 1890s had significant effects *(Crowther, M.A.)*. Women became eligible for election as Guardians and did much to humanise the Poor Laws. They became particularly important in encouraging the removal of children entirely from the workhouse and their accommodation with foster parents, or in smaller Scattered Homes. They also took a special interest in raising nursing standards in the infirmaries, and the care of the old people. Working class Guardians and others of radical or socialist ideas also became eligible for election, speeding up the pace of change and encouraging the kinder treatment of inmates.

Charity and the original 1834 Act were not very compatible bedfellows and it was only due to the efforts of reformer Louisa Twinning and the Workhouse Visiting Society in 1858 that regulations started to become more humane. From 1885 workhouse discipline was slowly relaxed. Guardians could buy books or newspapers for the aged (1891), toys for the children (1891), tobacco and snuff for the elderly (1892), dry tea, with sugar and milk for deserving inmates to brew at will (1893), and piano or harmonium for services and entertainment (1904) *(Crowther, M.A.)*.

In 1909 the Government introduced old age pensions, and the effect was almost immediate on reducing new admissions to the workhouse to only helpless old people who had no one to look after them *(Longmate, N.)*. In the same year a network of labour exchanges was set up to help anyone without work find a job. Unemployment insurance came in 1911.

The condemning report in 1909 of the Royal Commission on Poor Laws could not be ignored by the Local Government Board. In particular, it criticised the debilitating effect of workhouse life on the character of inmates, and deplored the forced mixing of reputable and disreputable poor. Regulatory changes swiftly followed *(Crowther, M.A.)*.

An Order in 1913 relaxed many central regulations to allow greater local discretion. The local Union Board could make its own regulations for searching and classifying inmates, for prohibiting certain articles, for mealtimes, for times of work, rising, and sleep. The approval of workhouse diets had previously been relaxed in 1900, but now the further relaxation of dietary regulations was allowed. In essence, the workhouse officials and Guardians were largely freed of detailed central control and were able to determine themselves the character of workhouse life. Other changes took place on the health front. All workhouse infirmaries were to have a properly qualified nurse, and the Medical Officer was required to examine all infants under the age of 18 months at least once a fortnight.

All these changes were further reflected in the changes in terminology in 1913 *(Crowther, M.A.)*. Workhouses were to have a change of image with a change of name. From then on they were to be called Poor Law Institutions, with inmates in their wards, and patients in their infirmaries. The Institutions were no longer intended only to deter the able bodied paupers, but they were to provide a refuge for the helpless and to fulfill a positive social purpose. Children were finally removed from them in 1915 when Guardians were banned from retaining any children over 3 years old for more than 6 weeks.

In 1919 the new Ministry of Health absorbed the Local Government Board and the Poor Law administration, intact and unchanged. The Great War removed the more able bodied paupers, but left the old, mentally defective, and helpless, little affected. Throughout the 1920s relief was provided by an uncoordinated mass of local authorities and charities in an unplanned network of specialised and unspecialised buildings *(Crowther, M.A.)*. During this period Guardians could foresee their powers passing to the public assistance committees of county and county borough councils. Their fate was sealed by the appointment of Mr Chamberlain as Minister of Health in 1923, and during the period 1924-29. He disliked Guardians, on account of their waste and muddle *(Crowther, M.A.)*. By the mid 1920s Chamberlain and his officials had agreed to reorganise local government to eliminate them. In 1929 their powers were formally transferred and local Unions, Boards and Guardians passed into history.

Former workhouses continued under the new regimes whilst their futures were discussed. Many continued to function caring for the old, the sick, and/or the mentally defective. Others were closed as part of cost-reducing reorganisations, and either passed into new uses, remained empty and derelict, or were demolished.

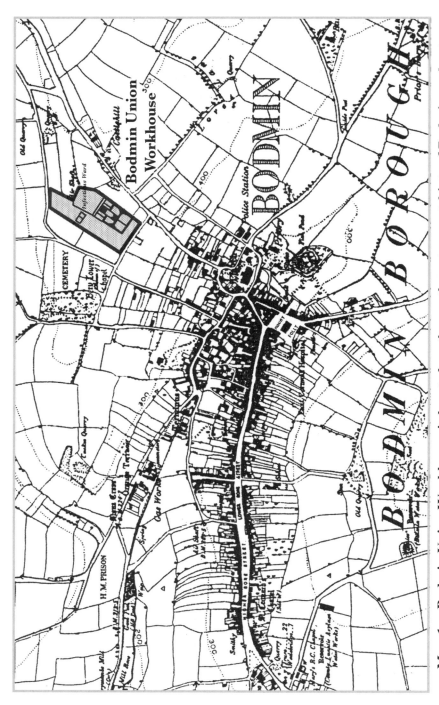

Map 1: Bodmin Union Workhouse is located on the north eastern outskirts of Bodmin, a short distance from the cemetery and Berry Tower. *(Adapted from 1880, 6" to 1 mile, Ordnance Survey Map)*

Chapter 3

The Inmates

The new workhouse, built on a site off Cemetery Lane on the eastern outskirts of Bodmin as indicated on *Map 1*, was formally certified by the Poor Law Commission on 20 November, 1842, with a capacity to accommodate a total of 250 paupers *(MH/12/1274)*.

Statistics in the Poor Law Commission files *(MH/12/1274 & MH/12/1275)* show that in the first 3 years, the average weekly numbers of paupers relieved by residing in the new workhouse were: 105 (1842); 117 (1843); 122 (1844).

The decennial censuses up to 1901 give more detailed statistics for the trends in numbers during the second half of the 19th century. Continuing after 1901 is not possible using the Census information which has yet to be published. However, referring to the statistics given in the local weekly newspaper reports, the Cornish Guardian, the following total numbers can be extracted for inmates in residence at similar times of year:

30 March 1851	149	3 April 1881	112	8 April 1910	117
7 April 1861	137	5 April 1891	64	28 January 1921	85
2 April 1871	159	31 March 1901	70	17 July 1930	70

Whilst these statistics give a general idea of the trend in inmate numbers over an 80 year period it must be remembered that numbers fluctuated significantly by the year, by the time of year, and even daily. Only an examination of the Master's attendance book would give the full story, and this is now no longer available. What the figures do appear to show is that numbers were lower in the second half of the workhouse's history, compared with the first half in the 1800s. Throughout its 94-year existence the workhouse was also always operating well below its total capacity to accommodate 250 inmates. Overcrowding was never a real problem in the Bodmin Union workhouse.

In the national context, the rural workhouses in the South west, such as Bodmin, were very modest in scale compared to those in London and the other large cities throughout the country. In March, 1851 the total number of indoor paupers in workhouses on census night was 126,488 *(Todd, A.)*; Cornish workhouses in total in January, 1861 held a total of 1,664 *(Bennett, A.)*, or 1.3% of the 1851 national total.

The following table *(Bennett, A.)* gives details of all the 13 workhouses in

Cornwall in 1861, and puts the Bodmin Union workhouse in 8th place at that time , as regards size by number of inmates:

Union	Parishes	1861 inmates
Stratton	11	20
Camelford	14	49
Launceston	25	68
St Germans	14	107
Liskeard	25	158
Bodmin	**21**	**137**
St Columb	16	93
St Austell	15	159
Truro	25	209
Falmouth	10	153
Helston	18	178
Redruth	8	210
Penzance	20	133

The population of the Bodmin Union increased only slightly over the period 1841-1931, averaging during this time about 19,250 (various *Kelly's Directories for Cornwall* in this period). The inhabitants of the workhouse averaged 107, or 0.6% of the resident population.

Paupers in total far exceeded the actual numbers in workhouses, due to the numbers who were still eligible for outdoor relief. In 1849 there was an overall total of 1,088,659 paupers of all classes, with only 133,513 (12%) in the workhouses, and the remainder, 955,146 (88%), receiving varying levels of relief outside workhouses *(Preston-Thomas, H.).* For Bodmin Union the ratio of indoor to outdoor paupers during the 1840s was roughly 1:4 *(MH/12/1275)-* by the early 1900s this proportion had risen as high as 1:8 on occasions *(Cornish Guardian reports).*

Analysis of the Census information during the 1800s gives a fascinating insight into the composition of the workhouse population during that century. It confirms a fundamental fact, that contrary to the intention of the original 1834 Act, the able bodied work shy poor for whom the workhouse system had been devised were never the predominant inmate group. Appendix 1 gives details from the 1881 Census returns of the officials and inmates in the Bodmin Union workhouse on the Census night, 3 April, 1881.

Each Census return, apart from 1881, shows that women inmates in the Bodmin workhouse outnumbered men.

Year	Men	Women		Year	Men	Women
1851	64	85		1881	57	55
1861	56	81		1891	26	38
1871	79	80		1901	34	36

Taking the men for 1851 and 1881, an analysis of their age structure shows a concentration at either end of the age range, compared to the mid ranges. The position with the women shows differently, with significant proportions in the middle age range.

Age range	1851		1881	
	Men	Women	Men	Women
0-15 yrs	34 *(53%)*	33 *(39%)*	32 *(56%)*	20 *(36%)*
16-65 yrs	13 *(20%)*	44 *(52%)*	13 *(23%)*	24 *(44%)*
+65 yrs	17 *(27%)*	8 *(9%)*	12 *(21%)*	11 *(20%)*

Details given in the Census returns on the social composition of inmates explain this difference. In 1851, 1 in 7 of the inmates was an unmarried mother in the Union workhouse with one or more children; in 1881 the figure was 1 in 9. The workhouse was the place of shame for the poor woman who had fallen from the moral high place of Victorian society.

Dr William Acton, a great authority on mid Victorian prostitution, wrote in 1857 - "...it cannot be denied by anyone acquainted with rural life, that the seduction of girls is a sport and habit with vast numbers of men, married and single, placed above the ranks of labourer....The "keeping company" of the labouring classes, accompanied by illicit intercourse, as often as not leads to marriage; but not so of the farmer's son, farmer, first or second or third class squire. The union house is now often enough the home of the deserted mother and infant bastard..." *(Longmate, N.)*

Typical entries in the Census records are:

1851
Frances Whetter	*20 yrs*	*Unmarried*	*Born Lanlivery*
Sarah Jane Whetter	*3 mth*	*Daughter*	*Born Bodmin*

1881
Susan Jones	*27 yrs*	*Unmarried*	*Born St Kew*
Elizabeth Ann Jones	*6 yrs*	*Daughter*	*Born St Kew*
Annie Jones	*1 yr*	*Daughter*	*Born Bodmin*

Analysis of the social composition shows how the largest group in the workhouse, the children, were made up.

Category	1851		1881	
Children (15 yrs or less)				
Unattached children	27	*(18%)*	24	*(21%)*
Children with unmarried mothers	29	*(20%)*	20	*(18%)*
Children with other parents	11	*(7%)*	8	*(7%)*
Total children	**67**	***(45%)***	**52**	***(46%)***
Adults				
Unmarried mothers	21	*(14%)*	12	*(11%)*
Married persons	12	*(8%)*	5	*(5%)*
Spinsters	19	*(13%)*	10	*(9%)*
Widows	5	*(3%)*	11	*(10%)*
Bachelors	11	*(7.5%)*	12	*(11%)*
Widowers	11	*(7.5%)*	10	*(9%)*
No information given	3	*(2%)*	--	
Total adults	**82**	***(55%)***	**60**	***(54%)***
Total persons	**149**	***(100%)***	**112**	***(100%)***

Unattachment to an adult for children usually arose in one of three ways - children being orphaned; children being abandoned by one or both parents; or children being removed to the workhouse as a way of relieving families outside, in lieu of giving actual financial relief. In 1851, 19 of the 27 unattached children (70%) were in the workhouse alone, without any brothers or sisters with them; in 1881, 11 of the 24 unattached children (46%) were alone.

Typical entries in the records of children being alone without parents in the Bodmin workhouse are:

1851

Elizabeth Philp	*12 yrs*	*Tailor's daughter*	*Born St Endellion*
Richard Philp	*10 yrs*	*Tailor's son*	*Born St Endellion*

1881

John Phillips	*7 yrs*	*Born Lostwithiel*
Millicent Phillips	*6 yrs*	*Born Lostwithiel*
William Phillips	*3 yrs*	*Born Lostwithiel*
Henry Phillips	*1 yr*	*Born Lostwithiel*

The age distribution of the children is shown in the analysis of the records for 1851.

Age	Boys	Girls
Under 1 yr	4 *(12%)*	3 *(9%)*
1 - 5 yrs	9 *(26%)*	8 *(24%)*
6 - 10 yrs	13 *(38%)*	14 *(43%)*
11 - 15 yrs	8 *(24%)*	8 *(24%)*

Beyond the age of 15 the records for each Census year show a sharp decrease in the numbers of adolescents still residing in the workhouse, with minimum numbers of 16-20 year olds. By that age Guardians had been anxious to relieve the ratepayer of continuing to support workhouse children and made every attempt to make them independent. Boys commonly became agricultural labourers, apprentice tradesmen such as shoemakers or tailors, or joined the armed forces. Girls usually went into domestic service. Emigration to the new world countries of the Empire, such as Canada, Australia and New Zealand, was also encouraged, with the Guardians in many instances approving assistance with the payment of the sea passages.

In early 1909 a new Local Government Board Inspector, Mr E D Court, attended the Union Board meeting and presented his report on the workhouse. As far as the children in it were concerned he commented on the sharing of one day room and washing accommodation by a large number of boys, girls, and infants; the justification for a separate ward for children in the infirmary; and the removal of children entirely from the workhouse into a couple of cottage homes, as the St Austell Union had already done *(CG 12 March, 1909)*. In 1910 the Inspector found that nothing had been done and reported again on the greatly overcrowded children's quarters, with 33 children sleeping in 20 beds - a few days previously it had been 36 or 37 children in the same number of beds *(CG 14 Jan.,1910)*. A deputation of the Board duly visited St Austell where 3 scattered homes had already been successfully established. As a result of the visit it was decided as an experiment to proceed with establishing a cottage home for 12 girls in the first instance. No suitable properties could be found to rent in the town for this purpose. In June 1910 Lord Clifden indicated his willingness to sell a piece of land to the Board adjacent to the Old Soldiers DCLI Regimental homes off Beacon Road so that a purpose built scattered home could be erected *(CG 3 June, 1910)*. In October 1910 the Board agreed the plans for the new home, prepared by Mr W J Jenkins, Bodmin Rural District Council surveyor, at a total cost, excluding the land, not to exceed £500 *(CG 7 Oct.,1910)*. The lowest tender of the local builder C F Ham, for £435 to build the home, was accepted in October 1911 *(CG 20 Oct.,1911)*, and building works commenced, with the new home for 12 girls being opened in April, 1913 *(CG 18 April, 1913)*.

With regard to accommodation for the boys, in June 1914 the Local Government Board notified the Bodmin Union that it would not sanction a proposal by them to appropriate a part of the workhouse as a separate boys home *(CG 24 June, 1914)*. The Board required the boys to be out of the workhouse altogether, similar to the girls. Two advertisements for houses to rent produced no satisfactory results. At the end of 1914 the Guardians sought to persuade the Local Government Board to allow the matter to be postponed until after the war *(CG 11 Dec., 1914)*. The Board refused, indicating that the Bodmin Union should be treated no differently from other poor law unions in the South West *(CG 25 Dec., 1914)*. In 1915 a suitable house in Berrycombe Hill was procured for an initial period of 3 years at a rent of £35 per annum. The Local Government Board Inspector was prepared to certify it as suitable for 14 boys *(CG 19 Feb., 1915)*.

In the 2-year period 1913-1915 the provision of 2 scattered homes had enabled long stay children under the age of 15 years to be completely removed from the workhouse. In each home it was intended that foster mothers would be able to create a more suitable "family environment", and bring the children up as if they were their own, far away from the undesirable influences of workhouse adult inmates. The workhouse was left to house the sick, the old, and the few able bodied adults.

Returning to the workhouse in the 1890s, statistics in the reports by visiting Local Government Inspectors give a clear indication of the distribution of inmates, and on most occasions the degree of under occupation of the workhouse. Hence, Preston Thomas reported on 12 April 1897 *(MH/12/1295)* that there was plenty of room in the workhouse, as clearly shown by the occupancy figures which he recorded.

Beds (Occupied)			Beds (Occupied)		
Men			**Women**		
Able bodied	16	(--)	Able bodied	16	(15) *
Old men	8	(5)	Old women	16	(--)
Boys	24	(15)	Girls	16	(9)
Male infirmary	12	(6)	Female infirmary	20	(17)
Infectious ward	4	(--)	Lying in ward	3	(2)
Receiving ward	1	(--)	Infectious ward	4	(--)
			Receiving ward	1	(--)
TOTAL	65	(26)	TOTAL	76	(43)
			*Including 5 infants		

Returns 17 years earlier by the Inspector who visited on 27 September 1880

(MH/12/1284) confirm how the able bodied inmate was in the minority compared to children and the infirm, clearly at this time the house was being affected by a bout of fever:

Men		Women	
Able bodied	16	Able bodied	32
Old men	7	Old women	--
Boys	19	Girls	9
Male infirmary	14	Female infirmary	16
Male infectious	10	Lying in	2
Male receiving	4	Female infectious	10
		Female receiving	4
TOTAL	70	TOTAL	73

Finally, the census returns give insights into the previous occupations of inmates before entering the workhouse, and the parishes where they were born. Thus, in 1851 the range of occupations, the number of inmates (and spouses/children) was:

Agriculture				**Trades (continued)**		
Farm servant	28 (28)			Wheelwright	1	
Farm labourer	9 (11)			Barge man	1	
Farmer	1 (3)			Seaman	1	
Sub total: 80 54%				Dressmaker	1	(2)
Domestic Service				Carpenter	1	
House servant	10	(8)		Mason	1	(2)
Charwoman	5	(3)		Tanner	1	
Gardener	1			Woolcomber	--	(1)
Sub total: 27 18%				Painter	--	(4)
Mining				Malster	--	(1)
Stream tinner	3	(4)		Engraver	--	(1)
Sub total: 7 5%				Tailor	--	(2)
Trades				Sub total: 30 20%		
Shoemaker	2	(5)		Vagrant	1	
Innkeeper	1			No information given	4	
Miller	1			Sub total: 5 3%		
Brazier	1					

All inmates: 149 100%

The information regarding places of birth of inmates in the Bodmin Union workhouse in 1851 confirms the relatively static nature of the population at that time. Whilst the laws preventing the movement of people seeking work, and in times of hardship seeking relief, in parishes other than their birthplace, had been lifted by the mid 1800s, each Union nevertheless endeavoured to relieve only its own population. Newcomers into the Union area were, if possible, when seeking relief referred back to the Union of their previous residence in order to avoid the cost to local ratepayers.

The places of birth of the inmates present in the Bodmin workhouse on the date of 1851 census were:

Within the Bodmin Union		Outside the Bodmin Union	
Bodmin Borough	17	Within Cornwall	19
Bodmin parish	17	Outside Cornwall	4
Blisland	4	Not stated	5
Cardinham	3		
Egloshayle	20		
Lanivet	2		
Lanlivery	9		
Lostwithiel	5		
Luxulyan	9		
St Endellion	9		
St Kew	9		
St Mabyn	9		
St Minver Highlands	3		
St Minver Lowlands	1		
St Winnow	3		
Withiel	1		
Sub total	121 *(81%)*	Sub total	28*(19%)*

Inmates in the main house and infirmary were regarded as permanent residents in the workhouse, even although their numbers varied from day to day, as well as their lengths of stay. Guardians were always grateful to see them return to independence outside off the Union books, and inmates occasionally were glad of a change to the outside world in order to escape the daily drudgery of the workhouse confines. However, their transience was never the same as the other group of workhouse visitors - the casuals.

This was the term used to cover those who were otherwise called vagrants, tramps, or men of the road. The majority were men, with a minority of women, and even occasionally children.

They were of no fixed abode, had no employment, rarely any family connections, and no roots in any particular place. Some were genuinely moving around in an endeavour to find work, but the majority were just hopeless drifters seeking to avoid work. Parish relief and the workhouse provided a daily meal, and a shelter overnight. Some had definite parts of the country which they trudged around, varying perhaps according to the time of year; others just wandered aimlessly, walking about 20 miles daily from one workhouse to the next.

Prior to the beginning of the 20th century the number of casuals in Devon and Cornwall was very limited. Shortly after opening in 1842 the records for Bodmin show 15 men and 9 women casuals relieved at the workhouse during the week ended 19 December 1846 *(MH/12/1275)*. On inspections of the workhouse in September 1880 4 men and 4 women casuals were recorded as present *(MH/12/1284)*; in May 1899 3 men and 3 women casuals *(MH/12/1295)*. Local Government Inspector Preston Thomas notes in his lifetime recollections that "...in 1896 west of the Tamar tramps are virtually non existent. This is due largely to the vigorous measures adopted by the late Chief Constable of Cornwall who harried them so much if they begged, that they soon gave him and his county a wide berth" *(Preston-Thomas, H.)*.

However, at the beginning of the 20th century all this changed and tramps started coming westwards in increasing numbers, possibly related to smallpox epidemics in London shortly after the turn of the century. In 1906 the Bodmin Union Board requested the Master to report on the numbers of tramps calling at the workhouse during the first 6 months of the year - totals of 283 men, 17 women, and 4 children had been recorded, with 6 men being admitted twice and 1 man three times; 1 woman had been admitted three times and another twice. The total figure had averaged out at 12 casuals per week to accommodate. In terms of composition, 176 of the men were classed as labourers, with the remainder representing 43 different callings; 69% were men aged 20-50 years of age *(CG 14 Sept.,1906)*.

The trend continued upwards, with a record reported in February 1909 of 105 tramps passing through during the past fortnight *(CG 26 Feb., 1909)*. A year later the Master presented to the Board more detailed statistics on numbers of casuals calling *(CG 25 Feb.,1910)*:

Year	Men	Women	Children	Total
1905	554	26	8	588
1906	700	20	15	735
1907	905	36	9	950
1908	1351	55	12	1418
1909	2162	69	17	2248

Bodmin was lucky in not being one of the unions on the border with Devon where even higher figures were recorded as tramps crossed the Tamar from England - at Launceston in 1906, 1580 tramps were recorded, compared to

Bodmin's 735 *(CG 23 Nov., 1906)*.

Police records showed that the number of tramps in Cornwall as a whole had increased from 1305 to 16,200 in the first 9 years of the century *(CG 25 Feb., 1910)*.

The problems posed by accommodating this high number of casuals, 70-80 a week on occasions, in a workhouse with maximum provision for 16 at any one time, continued to concern the Union Board until the outbreak of the Great War in 1914. Soon after that numbers dropped dramatically as casuals enlisted or filled jobs vacated by the resident population going to war. On 16 April 1915, only 29 tramps were reported for the past fortnight, compared to 91 in the same period the previous year. In 1917 the Local Government Board approved the proposal by the Bodmin Board to close the casual wards at the workhouse as numbers had dropped as low as 12 for a fortnight *(CG 8 June, 1917)*.

After the end of the War, and during the 1920s, numbers of casuals slowly began to increase again, probably due to rising unemployment, and the casual wards were re-opened. In August 1922, 100 tramps were recorded as passing through the casual wards in the past fortnight, and the Guardians passed a motion urging the Government to deal with the vagrancy question by the establishment of labour colonies, or Government works, where vagrants could be usefully employed. In Bodmin it was suggested by one Guardian, Mr W Phillips, that "...the old prison could be re-opened as a kind of national workshop for tramps..." *(CG 11 Aug., 1922)*.

1819 casuals were recorded during the whole of 1922, compared to only 815 for 1921 *(CG 17 Nov., 1922)*. Whilst discussions took place amongst all Cornish unions on how to devise a uniform system to deal with vagrants across the County, Bodmin Union was the only one which organised a scheme of labour tasks to be carried out by visiting casuals. In April 1924 the Master was able to report with some satisfaction that there had been a significant reduction in the number of tramps to 48 during the previous fortnight *(CG 18 April, 1924)*. Members of the Board felt that this was due to appropriate accommodation being provided for them, and the compulsory performance of tasks, not required at other places. On the road word spread along the "grapevine" to avoid Bodmin due to the poor accommodation as regards beds for tramps. Practically everywhere else better beds were available for casuals than at Bodmin workhouse. Another deterrent against visiting Bodmin was that local magistrates co-operated with the Union Board by giving a month's imprisonment, rather than 7 days, if tramps refused to do their allotted tasks.

Everything continued well, with numbers of casuals being maintained at significantly lower levels, 20-40 per fortnight, until the beginning of 1926, when a change in national regulations came into effect. The Casual Vagrancy Order, 1925, required that the tasks to be done by casuals were to be in future measured in terms of time to be allocated, rather than the quantity of work to be achieved. The Union Board felt that to put vagrants on a time charter was bound to pave a way to laziness. They made various unsuccessful lobbying attempts to have the new Order amended back to the old basis *(CG 8 Jan., 1926)*. As the Board had feared the numbers of visiting casuals quickly began to rise again *(CG 19 March, 1926)*. In June 1926, 52 tramps passed through in a fortnight, compared to 20 in the same period the previous year. Numbers, however, never reached the same levels as prior to the Great War, and at the beginning of 1927, whilst 73 tramps passed through in a fortnight, the Master was able to report to the Board that within a radius of 30 miles Bodmin had fewer tramps than the other Unions *(CG 7 Jan., 1927)*. So it continued until the casual wards finally closed, with numbers of casuals fluctuating above and below 50 per fortnight, but not returning to seriously high levels again.

Plate 1: Bodmin around 1900 looking from below the Beacon across the valley towards the north.

The workhouse site is outlined. The main buildings can be distinguished by the numerous chimney stacks. To the left of them is the single storey isolation ward with the workhouse garden to the front.

(Photograph: Hector Fitzpatrick Collection, Bodmin)

Chapter 4

The Officials

Staffing levels and their mix at the workhouse changed over the course of its 94-year history.

Throughout, however, there was the over-riding desire by the Guardians to keep numbers of officials, and thereby costs, to a minimum. Salary levels were also a constant source of tension between Guardians and officials. The Bodmin Union was not renowned for its generous salaries and the Bodmin workhouse was a stepping stone on more than one occasion for staff to move on to better paid positions in larger establishments elsewhere.

Tensions amongst the officials existed at various times, and there was a specific note made to this effect in the central staffing register held at the Poor Law Commission *(MH/9/3)*. The Master and Matron were the key players in determining the day to day efficiency, or otherwise, and the general atmosphere prevailing in the workhouse. Their tact, or lack of it, in dealing with other officials was crucial in deciding whether harmony, or friction and tension, was dominant.

At the outset in 1842 officials comprised the Master and Matron, schoolmistress and porter, all in residence with the 100-150 inmates. By the 1880s this complement had expanded to include the Master and Matron, schoolmaster, schoolmistress, nurse, and porter. When the workhouse school was closed at the end of the 1800s the two school teachers were replaced by a single industrial trainer, but this decrease was more than compensated for by extra nursing staff and an assistant matron.

Over the whole time of its existence staffing levels roughly doubled, from 4 to 8 staff resident at any one time in the workhouse.

Master & Matron

The Bodmin workhouse was served during its history by the following Masters and Matrons:

	Annual Salaries	
	Master	*Matron*
William and Sarah Truman Oct 1838 - June 1869	£45	£15

	Master	Matron
Henry and Alice Drew July 1869 - Oct 1871	£35	£20
Edwin and Elizabeth Stephens Oct 1871 - July 1878	£35	£20
Tom and Mary Whale June 1878 - Dec 1905	£35 - £40	£20 - £25
Tom and Marjorie (Daughter) Whale March 1906 - Dec 1911	£45	£22.10s.
Richard and Mary Benny Jan 1912 - Aug 1923	£40 - £60	£25 - £55
Mr & Mrs H F Benny Sept 1923 - 1936	£60 - £67.10s	£56 - £63.10s.

Sources: MH/9/3; CG 25 July,1919; CG 10 Aug.,1923; and PU/BOD/39.

The role of the Master was to generally organise, oversee, and manage the workhouse. He was held to account for all supplies, responsible for all central statistical data demanded, and given great power over other officials and inmates. Much of his day was spent in filling in forms and keeping records. In 1867 the Poor Law Board issued a General Order of Accounts which listed nearly 24 records to be maintained, often on a daily basis. Admission and Discharge books had 31 columns which had to be filled in every time a pauper was admitted or let out of the workhouse. The Provisions Expenditure Book required the Master to strike a balance between the number of inmates in the house, the weight of each type of food consumed, the amount remaining in store, and the amount of food wasted in cooking. Standard measures were even laid down and had to account for wastage. The Guardians could demand to inspect the books at any time and the district auditor was expected to do so four times a year *(May, T)*. Unfortunately, none of these records for the Bodmin workhouse exist any longer, and an invaluable insight into the details of daily life has been lost.

Whilst the Master carried out more of an overseers role, the Matron, his wife almost always, had a more practical approach, particularly in the early days of the workhouse. The domestic routine of the house was her primary concern. The kitchens and food preparation; the laundry and washing; the cleaning of the workhouse; and the supervision of the infirmary, were her key duties *(Crowther, M.A.)*. In carrying these out she relied for labour on the able bodied inmates, particularly the women. Before moves nationally in the last quarter of the 1800s to install trained nurses in the infirmary, the Matron also was responsible, with pauper assistance, for the nursing care, such as it was, in the workhouse hospital. Even after nurses began to be appointed to replace pauper nurses, the Matron would attempt to maintain her overall position over infirmary staff. Needless to say this often caused much ill feeling and dissent amongst the nursing staff so that turnover was the highest for all workhouse staff.

During its 94 years in existence the day to day running of Bodmin workhouse passed through the hands, in the main, of three families - initially, the Trumans (31 years); in the middle period the Whales (33 years); and, finally, the Bennys (24 years) *(MH/9/3)*.

The first Master and Matron were appointed by the Union Board soon after it had been established in 1837. The circumstances arose from a scandal concerning the previous Master and Matron at the temporary workhouse. The temporary workhouse, situated at the bottom of Crinnick's Hill, bridged the gap between the original poor house and the building of the new workhouse. It was managed by a William Congdon and his wife, Sarah. However, in 1838 charges were brought against them of embezzlement of stores, and misconduct against several of the female inmates. The Master was charged with misbehaviour and misconduct against Ann Gofs, Elizabeth Philp, and Ann Burrow. Magistrates found the pair guilty and fined them. The Union Board immediately dismissed them *(MH/12/1274)*.

William Truman and his wife Sarah were appointed in October 1838, following public advertisement and on the recommendation of the Assistant Poor Law Commissioner, Mr Gilbert, responsible for overseeing the formation of the new Unions in Devon and Cornwall *(MH/12/1274)*. They had previously been Master and Matron of a workhouse in Teignmouth, Devon, and came from there with good references. On appointment William was 39 years of age, and

[DUTY FREE.]

Bodmin Union.

WANTED, a MASTER and MATRON for the BODMIN UNION WORKHOUSE. Candidates are requested to send their applications and testimonials to me, on or before FRIDAY, the 28th instant, and to appear at the Meeting of the Guardians on the following day, at Twelve o'Clock.

The Salary will be £75 per Annum, with Coals and Candles.

W. R. Hicks,
Bodmin, September 19, 1838.   Clerk, &c.

Royal Cornwall Gazette

Sarah 43 years of age. They moved into the temporary workhouse initially with their two children, Henry, 7 years old, and Rosa, a baby. Their joint salary was £60/year, together with coals and candles being provided. However, in 1851 to reduce the costs to ratepayers of the new Poor Law system, the Guardians reduced their salary, along with that of other officers, to £47/year (MH/12/1276).

After supervising the early years of the new workhouse without appearing to attract too much criticism from Inspectors, time and age caught with the Trumans in 1869. By then Mrs Truman was 70 years old and the Poor Law Inspector, Mr Lougley, on his visit in March 1869 reported that "...the matron seems incapable through age and infirmity of satisfactorily discharging her duties...". She had become extremely deaf, and was being assisted in her duties by her daughter Rosa. Mr Lougley noted that on the other hand the Master "...appears vigorous and I saw no reason to doubt his efficiency. I understand however that complaints have been preferred against him..." (MH/12/1280).

No doubt under pressure from this report, and the subsequent reaction to it by the Guardians, the Trumans, albeit reluctantly in the absence of any pension provision at that time for workhouse officials, resigned as Master and Matron in June 1869 (MH/12/1280). They did not, however, immediately move out of the workhouse. On his next visit in September 1869 the Poor Law Inspector found them still in the workhouse, with Mrs Truman too ill to be moved. She subsequently died in the workhouse, and Mr Truman then was forced in due course to move elsewhere.

The Guardians proceeded to advertise for a new Master and Matron. In July 1869 they appointed one Henry Drew, 31 years old, and his wife Alice, 29 years old (MH/12/1280). They moved from Falmouth, with no children, where Mr Drew had been a carpenter by trade. However, for the last 8 years he had been the secretary of an Odd Fellows Lodge with some 450 members. His wife Alice had had some experience as a lodging house keeper. In addition to their joint salary of £55/year, they were also allowed a rations allowance.

Chaos followed their appointment. After his visit on 13 September 1869 the Poor Law Inspector wrote a letter to the Guardians expressing his concern at finding "...the workhouse in great disorder due to the absence of the master and schoolmaster through illness...". He noted that the Drews had been newly appointed, without any experience, and shortly after taking over, the Master had been attacked with fever, and had been unable to work ever since. His wife as Matron was also ill but had had the whole responsibility left to her. The Master had been given a month's absence to recover, and whilst the Matron had been authorised to find competent assistance, she had been unable to do so. The Inspector reported that the previous Master, Mr Truman, who was still living in the workhouse at that time, was supposed to be helping her, but "...he is worse than useless and reported to be a drunkard..." (MH/12/1280)

After this initial troublous introduction to workhouse life, the Drews clearly soon found their feet. In October 1871, only just over 2 years after their appointment, they resigned from Bodmin workhouse, Henry Drew having got himself elected as the Master of the Plymouth workhouse *(MH/12/1281)*.

The Drews were followed at Bodmin by the Stephens. Edwin Stephens had previously been a land surveyor and accountant, whilst his wife, Elizabeth, had had live-in experience as a housemaid and housekeeper *(MH/12/1281)*. The same age as the Drews, they were married and moved into the workhouse with a child of 9 months. Again, they must have quickly found their feet in running the workhouse as in 1878 they resigned their appointments after Edwin Stephens had been successful in being elected as Master of Swindon workhouse *(MH/12/1283)*.

There next followed the Whales, with Tom Whale being Master for the longest period in the history of the workhouse. Tom Whale had been born at Altarnun, and his wife Mary, at Helston. They moved from St Austell workhouse where Tom had been Master, and Mary had been schoolmistress *(MH/12/1283)*. Aged 30 and 29 years on appointment, they had, within 2 years of moving to Bodmin, two sons born, Banfield and Tom. By 1888 their family had grown to a total of 5 children, with two more sons, Arthur and Henry, and a daughter, Marjorie. A further daughter, Mary, arrived subsequently to complete the Whale family at the workhouse at the end of the 19th century.

After 24 years in service, personal problems beset the Whales, when at the age of 53 years, Mrs Whale was unable to continue her duties as Matron due to a heart complaint *(CG 7 Feb., 1902)*. In December 1905 she died and officially Tom Whale was forced to resign his position as Master *(CG 22 Dec., 1905)*. However, it seems likely that during the previous few difficult years their eldest daughter, Marjorie Whale, had been increasingly helping her father in the place of her mother - previously in 1901 the Board had agreed that she could be employed as a temporary assistant in the kitchens at a salary of £10 per year *(CG 5 April, 1901)*. Now on the death of Mary Whale, father and daughter were temporarily appointed as Master and Matron. This arrangement was confirmed in March 1906 *(CG 30 March, 1906)*.

By 1911 Tom Whale had reached the age of 63 years, and in the staff register is described as old and past active work *(MH/9/3)*. His daughter, Marjorie, tendered her resignation as Matron, having obtained the appointment as Matron at Shepton Mallett workhouse *(CG 22 Sept., 1911)*. It was agreed that the younger daughter, Mary Whale, would take over as Matron at Bodmin until Tom Whale finally retired as Master at the end of 1911 after 33 years as Master *(CG 6 Oct., 1911)*. On his retirement he moved to be with his eldest daughter at Shepton Mallett where the records note that he acted temporarily for the Master there during the period of the Great War whilst the latter was away on military service *(MH/9/3)*.

Immediately on the Whales resignation, Mr & Mrs Richard Benny wrote to the Board applying for the vacant posts of Master and Matron *(CG 3 Nov., 1911)*. Richard Benny, aged 58 years, had been at the workhouse for 16 years previously as porter. Mrs Benny had taken over from the last schoolmistress, Grace Pooley, in March 1897 as Industrial Trainer, responsible for the children. She had also acted as assistant matron and nurse. The Union Board impressed by their service, agreed that they should be appointed as the new Master and Matron, effective from January, 1912 *(CG 17 Nov., 1911)*.

Having been appointed at a much older age than earlier Masters, the length of service by the Benny's was inevitably shorter. They resigned on account of age in August 1923 *(CG 10 Aug., 1923)*. Their influence on the lives of the workhouse inmates, particularly the children, must have been considerable, and it appears that they were well liked. Signing himself "A Bodmin Boy, Twenty Years Ago", an old boy from the workhouse, after reading of the retirement of Mr & Mrs Benny, probably in the local newspaper which had been sent to him at his navy post in India, wrote a letter back to the paper expressing his appreciation of them:

"Feeling that I am expressing the thoughts of so many of the old boys and girls of your Institution, I would like to convey to your retiring Master and Matron our deepest gratitude for the valuable training we received whilst under their care, and for the love and sympathy with which they entered into our careers. The ratepayers have had full value for their money as regards the boys and girls Mr & Mrs Benny fitted out for their battle with life. It was their boys and girls who won so many prizes from the Bodmin Board School (now the County Council) and it is their boys and girls who are proving themselves valuable citizens of our Empire. An old boy myself, I know them, and I know that they have made good in Canada, New Zealand, Australia, USA, and different parts of England where they have made their homes. Many of us are still as one family who write regularly to Mr & Mrs Benny receiving valuable help and advice in return, and we also visit and are visited by them when it is possible. No wages could ever pay for their unofficial work and their keen desire to be of some assistance to the boys and girls who were once under their care. No morning newspaper speaks of this and no doubt it is the last thing they would wish for, but, today, here at Calcutta, as I read of their retirement it moves me to strive to express a little of what they have both meant in my life and I am sure all of our childhood feel the same...." (CG 7 March, 1924)

The Board resolved to advertise for a new Master and Matron *(CG 10 Aug.,*

1923). Eight applications were received and five were selected for interview, including Mr & Mrs H F Benny, the son and daughter in law of the retiring Master and Matron *(CG 24 Aug., 1923).* The reasons for the decision by the Board to select the Bennys junior are not clear from the limited information available, but one can speculate that the standing and influence of their parents, the local connection, and the lobbying of Board members, were all factors which came into play. There was concern locally that unqualified and inexperienced applicants had been appointed *(CG 7 Sept., 1923).* The Ministry of Health questioned why applicants with no previous experience in poor law service had been appointed. Similar correspondence was received from the National Poor Law Officers Association. The Board left it to the skills of their Clerk to successfully explain and defend their decision *(CG 5 Oct., 1923).*

Despite these initial misgivings about the appointment, the Bennys junior seem to have quickly found their feet and made a success of their positions. Perhaps Mrs Benny might have been more diplomatic in her handling of other staff, particularly her assistants and the nursing staff. The Union Board in 1929 established a Committee to investigate the high number of resignations by assistant nurses and matron's assistants - in the previous 2 years 12 assistants in these posts had resigned *(CG 12 Sept., 1929).* The Committee concluded that the fault lay with the Matron who had displayed insufficient kindness and thought for the staff *(CG 24 Oct., 1929).* Despite this censure, the Board took no formal action against Mrs Benny, and both the Bennys remained in post at the workhouse until its closure in 1936.

Medical Officer

Medical Officers contracted by the Bodmin Union Board to serve the workhouse included:

	Dates	Annual Salary
John Ward	March 1856 - Sept 1865	£23.17s
Thomas Mudge	Oct 1865 - Sept 1868	£23.17s
Thomas Mudge	Dec 1868 - Sept 1871	£56
Bartholomew Derry	Sept 1871 - Nov 1911	£56
John Bawden	Dec 1911 - Jan 1916	£60
A Salmon	Jan 1916 - 1922	£95-£114
N Salmon	1922 - 1930	£100-£120

Sources: MH/9/3; and PU/BOD/39

Second in importance to the Master of the workhouse was the Medical Officer. He did not reside in it, but visited with varying frequencies, and was, in theory at least, responsible to the Master for the overall health of the inmates - both those actually sick in the infirmary, and those living in the main house *(Crowther, M.A.)*. Health care was basic, if at all, especially in the early years, and before the links between public health, personal health, and personal hygiene, had been established and accepted. It was 1899 before the notification of infectious diseases was introduced *(Preston-Thomas, H.)*. Extra fees could be charged for smallpox vaccinations, midwifery, and certain surgical operations, but if the Board of Guardians, to whom Medical Officers were contracted, refused to pay them, medical care was further minimalised *(Crowther, M.A.)*.

Bodmin Union was divided into 7 medical districts, and by 1844 Medical Officers had been contracted by the Board with responsibilities for each *(PU/Bod/1)*. Bodmin workhouse was included in District 3, under the care of a John Ward. Little detail is available from surviving records concerning him, other than he resigned from his post in 1865 due to age and infirmity *(MH/9/3)*.

Thomas Mudge, who succeeded him, had two spells as Medical Officer. Inadequate payment by the Guardians appears to have been the central issue leading to his first resignation in 1868, and subsequent reappointment. Initially the Board had refused to pay any extra fees to the Medical Officer's basic salary, and the resignation in 1868 is recorded as being on the grounds of his salary being too small. Even although a significant increase in salary was paid to Dr Mudge on his reappointment in 1868, his resignation in 1871 was again on the grounds of inadequate pay *(MH/9/3)*.

This financial stringency by the Guardians no doubt contributed towards the poor health conditions in the workhouse at this time. The general disorder found by the Poor Law Inspector on his visit in September 1869 was due to illness *(MH/12/1280)*. Fever had obviously taken a grip on the house, due in the Inspector's view to the most offensive cesspools in the vicinity of the house. There was no means of separating those sick with the fever from the general sick, with no separate infectious hospital building having yet been agreed. The Medical Officer had clearly not had any great impact at this time.

Following the resignation of Thomas Mudge in September 1871, the duties of the Medical Officer passed to one Bartholomew G Derry for the next 40 years from 1871-1911 *(MH/9/3)*. Records indicate that on average he visited the workhouse 3 times a week, as well as when specifically sent for *(MH/12/1284)*. It appears that, as was common at that time, record keeping was not his strongest point. The Local Government Inspector Preston Thomas noted on his visit in April 1897 that a record book was not being properly kept in the infirmary *(MH/12/1295)*. Another report at the end of 1897 further criticises the Medical Officer for his standards of care, administration, and the general state of the workhouse infirmary. With regards to the children in the workhouse this report mentions that their condition is not altogether satisfactory. There is no bathing accommodation for them. Some of their boots are too small for their feet. There are clearly cases of eye squints which should have been brought to the attention of the Medical Officer, and indeed would have been if he had been carrying out periodic inspections of the children which would have been most desirable. One particular boy, Chas Dawe, aged 8 years, had a growth on the alveolar process of the jaw, and this case should have received the attention of the Medical Officer *(MH/12/1295)*. In the central staffing register held by the Local Government Board there were notes written against the details for Dr Derry indicating that he neglected to report on the nursing arrangements, books, and inaccuracies in the medical reference book, as well as not observing the regulations in the Dietary Order of 1900 *(MH/9/3)*.

In November 1911 Dr Derry resigned, apparently on the grounds of age rather than dismissal for his lax ways, as the central staff register indicates that he was able to take advantage of the recently introduced superannuation provisions to secure a pension (MH/9/3). He was succeeded by John Bawden who was Medical Officer to the workhouse for 5 years before he died in January 1916. He obviously inherited the shortcomings left by his predecessor. The Local Government Inspector Mr E D Court visited the workhouse on 14 February 1912 and subsequently issued a critical report to the Guardians. He considered that there was "...a need to bring the infirmary more in line with up to date institutions with regard to numbers of nursing staff and equipment"*(CG 23 Feb., 1912)*. He was also critical of other matters, such as conditions in the casual wards, conditions in the main house for the children, and personal washing arrangements, all matters on which the Medical Officer might have been expected to be advising. Dr Bawden must have attended to the infirmary deficiencies without delay because on his next visit in September 1912 Inspector Court reported that "...the infirmary is in good order and nursing satisfactory" - inadequate washing though remained a criticism *(CG 20 Sept., 1912)*.

Following the death of Dr Bawden, the post of Medical Officer passed to the Salmons *(MH/9/3)*. Dr Salmon Senior held the post for 6 years until 1922, and was then succeeded by his son, Dr Norman Salmon.

Records are limited to the regular reports on workhouse affairs in the local newspaper during the 1920s and 30s, but those do not contain or infer any further serious criticisms of the workhouse infirmary, or medical care generally in the workhouse, under the Salmons. Furthermore, some heed had clearly been taken by the Guardians of the advice that greater numbers of nursing staff were required in the infirmary, as well as improvements to the washing facilities.

Schoolteacher

The central staff register for Bodmin workhouse records the following teachers who taught and looked after the children there between 1842 and 1895, when the children went out to the local day schools in the town:

Schoolmistresses	Dates	Annual Salary
Elizabeth Lawry	Sept 1842 - June 1867	£35
Lucilla Hicks	June 1867 - June 1873	£15
Laura Augusta Menhinnick	June 1873 - July 1878	£15
Marcia Smith	Aug 1878 - Nov 1880	£15
Grace Pooley	March 1887 - March 1895	£28-32
Schoolmasters		
Richard Lawry	Jan 1847 - Sept 1870	£35
William Jeffery	Sept 1870 - Dec 1876	£20
William Davey	Dec 1876 - Jan 188	£20

Source: MH/9/3

On the face of it the schoolteacher might be thought of as someone of status and profession amongst the staff living in the workhouse. However, such a thought derives from our knowledge of the school teaching profession long after teachers ceased to be employed in the Poor Law schools. Workhouse teachers existed in the era before it became compulsory in the 1880s that every child had to attend a school. In the outside world, illiteracy was the norm for the working classes, and only those who could afford the fees to attend the private schools which existed received any education. So, in that sense the workhouse child had an advantage with the workhouse school and its one or two teachers. This indeed was the intention of the Poor Law system that education, however basic, would assist in breaking the vicious cycle of poverty which otherwise continued through generations.

The standards of education for the 50 years or so that the system existed varied enormously, but were rarely beyond the basic reading, writing, arithmetic, and religious instruction. Teachers themselves had had no formal training in most cases and merely did their best to pass on the literacy skills which they had been lucky to acquire in their own lives. It was the efforts of the Poor Law Board which led to some improvement in workhouse education. Schools were inspected by the Board Inspectors on their visits to the workhouse, and teachers were examined annually themselves to determine their levels of competency. The latter in turn was the basis on which their salaries were determined, since the central Board contributed 50% towards them.

The Poor Law Commission had intended in the workhouse system that there should be a strict segregation of the sexes at all times and for all purposes. However, this intention was often not achieved in practice, particularly in the smaller, rural workhouses. In the Bodmin workhouse education of the children for the first 5 years from opening in 1842 was under the care of one teacher, Elizabeth Lawry.

In 1847 she was joined by her husband, and they taught the children in the schoolroom, with a curtain dividing the boys from the girls *(MH/12/1280)*. Elizabeth Lawry received an adverse report from the Assistant Poor Law Commissioner, Edward Gulson, who on his first visit to Bodmin in June 1847 considered her to be inefficient. He felt that "...a more efficient and better qualified schoolmistress should be appointed" *(MH/12/1275)*.

Despite this report, the Lawrys continued and in November, 1856 Mr Gulson was able to report that the school was now managed satisfactorily. The only criticism on that visit was against Mr Lawry, whom the Inspector commented "...does not sufficiently look after the boys after school hours...", as some of the boys were apparently being allowed to mix with the men *(MH/12/1277)*. However, in 1860 the workhouse school was reported as being in a satisfactory state and a credit to Mr Lawry *(MH/12/1278)*.

Schoolteachers were expected to do more than just teach workhouse children. They had to live at the workhouse and supervise the children at all times. School teaching was quite literally a 24 hours a day, 7 days a week, 52 weeks a year job. For this, rations and accommodation came to be regarded an essential part of their remuneration. To the extent that, after the Lawrys had resigned, the salaries of their successors were reduced in amount to reflect the living expenses which they received in kind.

In 1880, the Local Government Inspector found that under schoolmaster Davey, the boys school was well managed, but as far as the girls were concerned, whilst they were clean, Marcia Smith was not considered to be very competent or up to the job *(MH/12/1284)*. After she had resigned in November, 1880, the Guardians decided not to appoint another schoolmistress, but to put the boys and girls together under schoolmaster Davey *(MH/12/1284)*. This situation remained until January 1887, when William Davey resigned in order to become the Master of St Columb workhouse. The Guardians had to make another decision on what to do for the children. After much deliberation, they decided to leave the boys and girls together, and to advertise for a certified schoolmistress who would be required to carry out both school teaching duties and industrial training, as well as general supervision of the children during out of school hours *(MH/12/1289)*. Grace Pooley was subsequently appointed, at an enhanced salary to reflect the combined duties. She remained in post as schoolmistress until 1895, when the children were sent out to the Board schools in the town. Thereafter, she stayed for another 18 months as the Industrial Trainer, at a reduced salary of £25/year, plus rations and accommodation, before she resigned, and her duties were taken over by the porter's wife, Mrs Richard Benny *(MH/12/1295)*.

Porter

Porters recorded as serving at Bodmin workhouse are:

	Dates	Annual Salary
John Mitchell	Feb 1847 - Dec 1886	£22
John Lander	Dec 1886 - Dec 1890	£22.4s
Richard Pearse	Jan 1891 - May 1895	£22.4s
Richard Benny	June 1895 - Jan 1912	£30
Mr A Smith	Jan 1912 - Oct 1913	£27.10s
Mr W H Green	Oct 1913 - Feb 1917	£25
Mr E Hill	March 1917 - 1936	£25-£42.10s

Sources: MH/9/3; and PU/BOD/39

The porter was effectively the "keeper of the gate" at the workhouse, and was responsible for receiving, in the first instance, all those who called at the front door of the workhouse seeking relief. Those seeking on-going relief were directed to the receiving wards, after having been searched for any alcohol and tobacco *(Crowther, M.A.)*. There they awaited their fate pending their circumstances being considered by the Guardians at the next appropriate Board meeting. The other callers, who undoubtedly gave porters more problems, were the casual poor - the tramps and vagrants. Viewed with contempt by the porter, physical abuse and violence was often associated with the casuals *(Longmate, N)*. Added to which, it was one of the porter's duties to supervise them in performing their allotted tasks as payment in kind for their night's shelter. All in all the porter's life was not an easy one, and most in status were only slightly above the level of the pauper for whom they were responsible.

The first porter at Bodmin workhouse, who remained in post for 39 years, was John Mitchell, a Bodmin man by birth and a shoemaker by trade. He lived in two rooms in the front building adjoining the entrance, with his wife and two children *(MH/12/1275)*. Aged 30 years old when appointed as porter in 1847, he died in the workhouse at his post, in December, 1886, aged 69 years old *(MH/12/1288)*.

The next two porters, John Lander and Richard Pearse, served a much shorter period of 4 years each, with Richard Pearse being dismissed in May, 1895 for misconduct *(MH/12/1293)*.

Richard Benny was elected next, and must have served as porter with distinction, because after 17 years service he and his wife went on to be appointed Master and Matron. Aged 41 years old on becoming porter, he came from Newlyn East in Cornwall and was a boot/shoe maker by trade *(MH/12/1293)*. In fact most of the porters had this background and no doubt a considerable amount of their time was spent in tending to the footwear of the inmates, especially the children. A further requirement in the advertisement for his successor was that the porter should also be able to act as the barber for the inmates - workhouse haircuts were always severe and served as one of the distinguishing features which marked out workhouse children when they went into the outside world.

Beginning with the Bennys, the wife of the porter began to formally undertake paid duties in the workhouse as the loss of the schoolteachers for supervising the large numbers of children was felt. Mrs Benny started with general duties in the house, but in March 1897, was appointed as Industrial Trainer after the resignation of the last schoolmistress, Grace Pooley *(MH/12/1295)*.

The Smiths replaced the Bennys, each undertaking similar duties as the Bennys, but they only stayed just over 18 months. Applicants for workhouse posts were now being drawn from wider afield than during the previous century, and the Smiths had moved to Cornwall from Newhaven, Sussex *(CG 29 Dec., 1911)*. They resigned from Bodmin, having been offered similar positions in the workhouse at Eastbourne.

William Green, from Boconnoc, Lostwithiel, who followed Mr Smith, served just over 3 years before he was dismissed for his involvement with a suicide in the workhouse. Inmate Richard Pascoe Brown was found dead in the porter's quarters with a rubber tube attached to a gas jet clenched between his teeth. It was considered that the porter had had an involvement in it warranting his dismissal *(CG 16 Feb., 1917)*.

A local couple was appointed, following this misfortune - Mr & Mrs E Hill from Wadebridge *(CG 16 March, 1917)*. Whilst Mr Hill was appointed as porter, Mrs Hill was initially the Matron's assistant, and later the Industrial Trainer for the inmates. Both remained in post for almost 20 years until the closure of the workhouse for inmates in 1936.

Porter Hill clearly had his difficult experiences with the casuals calling at the workhouse. In September, 1925, 2 tramps, Ernest Yates, a 51 year old pedlar, and Frederick Morris, a 24 year old seaman, were brought to Bodmin

Police Court. Yates was charged with refusing to comply with workhouse regulations, using bad language, and threatening an officer; Morris was charged with absconding from the workhouse before completing his allotted task. It was reported in the court that Yates had got abusive with the porter, Mr Hill, after refusing to give up the food he was carrying when calling at the workhouse for overnight entry to the casual ward. Having walked from St Columb that day, he had bought cooked tripe in the town which he wanted to eat with the bread to be given to him in the workhouse. Magistrates found him guilty of the charges, but the penalty was not very effective as he was sentenced to 1 day's imprisonment which effectively meant an immediate discharge! *(CG 25 Sept., 1925)*

Nurse

The register of nurses serving at Bodmin workhouse is the longest, and would be even longer if it were complete with appointments in the 1920s which are missing:

Nurse	Dates	Annual Salary
Ann Giddy	? - Jan 1870	
Rebecca Hall	Feb 1870 - Feb 1872	£15
Mary Richards	Feb 1872 - March 1879	£15
Elizabeth Tucker	March 1879 - March 1881	£15
Mary Lampier	April 1881 - Nov 1885	£15-£18
Mary Faraghan	Nov 1885 - Sept 1888	£15
Maria Lampier	Oct 1888 - March 1901	£15-£20
Mary Whiting	March 1901 - Nov 1904	£25
Margaret Smith	Dec 1904 - Dec 1911	£25-£27.10s
Hilda Coleman	Feb 1912 - April 1913	£30.1s.35d
Lily Johnson	May 1913 - Dec 1924	£30.1s.35d-£55
Assistant Nurse		
Frances Whiting	July 1904 - ?	Salary £18
Alice Burt	April 1912 - Jan 1913	£25
Ella Munro	Jan 1913 - Oct 1914	£20.1s.25d
Elizabeth Blowey	Jan 1921 - ?	£45

Source: MH/9/3

For a considerable time after the 1834 Act the need for nursing staff in the workhouse infirmaries was considered unnecessary. It was often argued that the type of patient in the workhouse did not need specialised attention. The Matron of the workhouse, with the help of unpaid pauper assistants, was considered perfectly adequate for dealing with the infirmary, regarded little more than an extension of the main house. In some cases outside, untrained assistance was recruited, and local working class widows in particular often assisted in the workhouse infirmary.

As the 1800s progressed, the Local Government Board urged Guardians to employ paid nurses, rather than unpaid paupers already in the workhouse, but they did not insist that they had to be trained. The Regulations in 1847 only stated that " no person shall hold the office of nurse who is not able to read the directions on medicines " ! *(May, T)*. Workhouse nursing did not attract ladies or nurses trained in the outside voluntary hospitals, but attracted girls of the lower middle classes, daughters of professional men, farmers, and shopkeepers *(Crowther, M.A.)*. Rates of pay were never as high as in the voluntary hospitals, and decent living quarters were rarely offered. The positions were most likely to be taken by working class girls in preference to domestic service *(Crowther, M.A.)*.

This appears to have been the position for nurses in the Bodmin workhouse. No paid nurse was appointed for the first 20-25 years after the workhouse opened, and no nurse is listed amongst the workhouse staff recorded in the 1851 and 1861 census returns. After this when nurses started to be engaged their post was the lowest paid amongst the staff, and remained below that of the porter until the early 1920s. The low pay offered by the Bodmin Guardians appears to have been the reason on more that one occasion why nurses moved on to other better paid appointments elsewhere.

The early nursing arrangements, and the quality of staff, did not meet with the approval of the Local Government Board Inspectors. On his visit in September, 1880, the Inspector commented that the one paid nurse, Elizabeth Tucker, was too old for the work *(MH/12/1284)*. She apparently slept in the infirmary, with bells to wake her if sick inmates wanted her. Whether or not she always responded is open to question as in March 1881 she was dismissed for inefficiency *(MH/9/3)*. The report of Inspector Preston Thomas in April, 1897, confirms that Nurse Lampier was paid but untrained and continued to sleep in the infirmary *(MH/12/1295)*. He noted that the record book in the infirmary was not being properly kept. In December, 1897, the visiting Inspector castigated the Guardians in his report for continuing to employ pauper ward attendants in contravention of the recently introduced General Order banning them. He suggested that the services of a trained night nurse were required, and that the Medical Officer and nurse "...might with advantage adopt higher standards of administration for the sick wards" *(MH/12/1295)*

After the turn of the century, although workhouse nurses still felt somewhat isolated from the mainstream of their profession, conditions slowly improved for them as more importance was attached to nursing care in workhouses. At

Bodmin as numbers in the infirmary increased, an assistant nurse was recruited to ease the burden on the head nurse. Nurse Lily Johnson, who remained in post for 11 years as the longest serving nurse, 1913-1924, throughout the history of the workhouse, joined many other workhouse staff throughout the country on active military service during the Great War. In her absence special arrangements were made for temporary staff to cover her post until she returned *(MH/9/3)*.

After 1918, there was a gradual change in the nature of workhouse infirmaries as they moved more into line with outside general hospitals. The pay and conditions of nurses had to be improved dramatically in an endeavour to attract better calibre, trained nurses. At Bodmin the infirmary gradually changed, during the 1920s, into something more akin to a home for infirm, old (or elderly) persons, with the shame of the term pauper slowly disappearing. In 1927 it was agreed by the Guardians to engage an attendant for the mental defectives in the infirmary *(CG 4 March, 1927)*. In 1929, 22 years after the original recommendation in 1897, a night nurse was recruited *(CG 14 Feb., 1929)*.

The turnover of nurses, as indicated by the details reproduced from the central staff register, was the highest amongst all the staff employed in the workhouse. Reasons included poor pay and conditions, marriage, conflict with the workhouse Matron, and dismissal.

Dismissal occurred twice at Bodmin workhouse infirmary. Nurse Elizabeth Tucker as mentioned previously was dismissed in March 1881 for inefficiency. Nurse Mary Whiting was dismissed in November, 1904 for misappropriating money belonging to sick inmates *(MH/9/3)*.

The central staff register does not exist beyond 1921, but local newspaper reports give a flavour and indication of what happened in the 10 years beyond that date. They highlight what happened when the Matron of the workhouse continued to exercise her role of authority in the infirmary without tact and diplomacy for the nursing staff. Nurses came and went with increasing frequency from 1925 onwards. Some stayed a matter of months, others only a matter of weeks. A Committee set up by the Union Board in 1929 to investigate the reasons, concluded that the fault lay with the Matron who displayed insufficient kindness and thought for staff *(CG 24 Oct., 1929)*.

Chaplain

The 1834 Poor Law Amendment Act intended that the staff of each workhouse would include a chaplain to minister to the spiritual needs of the inmates. Most of the Cornish Unions never did this and chaplains were not appointed *(Crowther, M.A.)*. This included Bodmin where there was never any chaplain to the workhouse, despite an offer in December 1843 by a certain gentleman of the Union to provide one free for the ensuing year *(PU/BOD/1)*.

In the period between 1842 and 1900 there are two occasions when reports by visiting Inspectors refer to religious arrangements in the workhouse. In September, 1880 it is noted that "there were no Church of England services, but visits by a Church of England clergyman" *(MH/12/1284)* In April, 1897, Preston Thomas confirmed that there was no chaplain at the workhouse. He noted that "...a non conformist service is held once a week. There is no Church of England service but the vicar visits weekly, and at other times. The Church of England inmates might be allowed to go out to church if they wished. Children going to church do so in the morning (presumably on a Sunday, although he is not specific), and attend a non conformist service (presumably in the workhouse) in the afternoon" *(MH/12/1295)* It could well have been that these services were held in the old schoolroom, now disused for teaching purposes as the children were attending the local Board schools in the town.

There are only two other references in local newspaper reports to religion in the workhouse. In June, 1911, the House Committee of the Union Board considered that "... children from the house should not be allowed to attend Sunday Schools in the town as it would take them away from Sunday afternoon services at the workhouse, where they were so helpful with the singing" *(CG 16 June, 1911)*. In December, 1911, the local newspaper reported that Miss Mary Whale, the youngest daughter of Mr Tom Whale, who had just resigned as Master, had indicated she was willing to continue as organist at the Sunday services in the workhouse *(CG 1 Dec., 1911)*.

**Plate 2: William Robert 'Budley' Hicks (1808-1868).
Clerk to the Board of Guardians 1837-1868.**
(from Collier, W. F.)

Chapter 5

The Board Of Guardians

The implementation of the 1834 Poor Law Amendment Act in Cornwall, overseen by Assistant Poor Law Commissioner Gilbert, saw the County divided into 13 separate areas or districts, within which the parishes united to form Unions.

Union	No of Parishes	Date Commenced
Launceston	25	2 Feb 1837
Liskeard	25	16 Jan 1837
St Germans	14	14 Jan 1837
Bodmin	**21**	**10 May 1837**
Stratton	11	28 Jan 1837
Camelford	14	1 Feb 1837
St Columb	16	9 May 1837
St Austell	15	30 Apr 1837
Truro	25	12 May 1837
Falmouth	10	13 Jun 1837
Redruth	8	13 May 1837
Helston	18	12 Jun 1837
Penzance	20	10 Jun 1837

Source: Bennett, A.

Bodmin Union comprised 21 parishes and had a total population in 1831 of 18836. The parishes were:

Blisland	Lanhydrock	St Minver Highlands
Bodmin Borough	Lanivet	St Minver Lowlands
Bodmin parish	Lanlivery	St Tudy
Cardinham	Lostwithiel	St Winnow
Egloshayle	Luxulyan	Temple
St Endellion	St Kew	Warleggan
Helland	St Mabyn	Withiel

Source: Kelly's Directories of Cornwall (Various dates)

Each parish making up the Union was represented by one or more individuals, who were known as Guardians of the Poor, or in shortened form, Guardians. Initially, they were elected by the old Select Vestries which were replaced by

49

the new Unions, and many of the Guardians had previously served on these Vestries. As time passed these arrangements changed, and the rate paying public became involved so that Guardians were elected by them. By the end of the 1800s working class and women Guardians were being elected by rate payers with the right to vote *(Longmate, N.)*. In 1896 Bodmin Union had 4 lady members on the Board *(PU/BOD/4)*, and by 1927 this number had risen to 6 women Guardians, who were well regarded for their work to improve the conditions for the poor in the workhouse *(CG 27 May, 1927)*. On the other hand, changes to the Board, and the ways it carried out its business happened only very slowly *(Longmate, N.)*. There was often little interest at election times by those eligible to vote, and Guardians often stayed on the Board for many years - Richard Elford, member for St Tudy retired from the Board after some 50 years service, by the end of which he was referred to as "The Father of the Board", and a photograph of him was hung in the Board Room at the workhouse *(CG 29 April, 1927)*.

The majority of Guardians were also very parochial and limited in their views - as Preston Thomas observed "...one of the great faults of Guardians was that few took the trouble to gain any experience outside their own Unions, and took each case on its merits rather than applying any general principles" *(Preston-Thomas, H.)*. This situation did improve somewhat at the beginning of the 1900s with the Poor Law Conferences which were held annually at different centres in the west country, and allowed for an interchange of ideas between Board members and Clerks of Boards.

Bodmin Union had 37 elected Guardians *(Kelly's Directory, 1873)*. In addition, magistrates living in the Union were entitled to be ex officio Guardians *(MH/12/1274)*. In total there were some 52 Guardians who formed the Bodmin Union Board. This number varied over the years as arrangements for numbers of seats per parish changed, and numbers of magistrates changed.

The record of Guardians elected in April, 1849, to serve on the Board gives an indication of its composition, and the type of person involved in poor law work in the early days. The table on page 51 shows the record of guardians elected in April, 1849 to serve on the Board. It gives an indication of its composition and the type of person involved in poor law work in the early days. In summary: 16 yeomen; 8 farmers; 5 clerks (clergymen); 3 gentlemen; 2 merchants; 1 solicitor; 1 woolstapler; 1 lieutenant RN.

The responsibilities of each Union for its own area included public health (vaccinations and medical officers); registration of births and deaths; marriages; out relief of the poor; and the administration of the workhouse *(Kelly's Directory, 1888)*.

Parish	Guardian Elected	Profession
Blisland	Thomas Tom	Yeoman
Bodmin Borough	John Wallis	Clerk
	John Grose	Gentleman
	James Liddell	Lieutenant, RN
	Alfred Taylor	Clerk
Bodmin Parish	Thomas Mills	Farmer
Cardinham	John Vivian	Clerk
	William Henwood	Yeoman
Egloshayle	William Pollard	Yeoman
	Henry Vercoe	Yeoman
St Endellion	Mark Guy	Yeoman
	James Stephens	Merchant
Helland	Henry Hooper	Gentleman
Lanhydrock	Samuel Johns	Farmer
Lanivet	James Retallick	Yeoman
	Anthony Knight	Farmer
Lanlivery	F Kendell	Clerk
	John Phillips	Yeoman
	William Lyttleton	Yeoman
Lostwithiel	Christopher Arthur	Merchant
	Robert Nicholls	Wool Stapler
Luxulyan	John Barnicot	Farmer
	James Nankevil	Farmer
St Kew	William Grose	Yeoman
	Nicholas Hawke	Yeoman
St Mabyn	George Somerset	Clerk
	Abraham Hambly	Gentleman
St Minver Hghlds	Henry Symons	Yeoman
	John Beswetherick	Yeoman
St Minver Lwlds	Simon Willcock	Yeoman
St Tudy	George Stephens	Yeoman
	Nathaniel Stephens	Yeoman
St Winnow	Edmund Facey	Farmer
	Thomas Wevell	Farmer
Temple	John Collins	Solicitor
Warleggan	Thomas Runnals	Farmer
Withiel	John Sobye	Yeoman

Source: Poster giving election results, Hector Fitzpatrick Collection, Bodmin.

In 1894 Rural District Councils were formed to take over from parishes the remaining responsibilities which they had retained after the 1834 Poor Law Amendment Act - these included such matters as public health (foul drainage systems) and highways *(CG 11 March, 1937)*. Bodmin Rural District, which later disappeared in the 1930s with another Local Government re-organisation, comprised the same parishes as in the Union, with the exception of Bodmin Borough, Lostwithiel, and Wadebridge, which each managed their affairs independently. The same members elected to serve the Union also served the Rural District Council, and the meetings of both took place in the workhouse *(Kelly's Directory, 1914)*.

Bodmin Union Board meetings took place in the Board Room in the workhouse on alternate Saturday mornings or afternoons. The Board relied on a system of Committees, which met at other times in the workhouse, to carry out its detailed business, with Committee reports being placed before the full Board meetings for discussion and ratification. These Committees varied in number and composition over the years, for example, the Committees to which Guardians were elected after the elections in April 1919 were:

Finance Committee	15 seats
House Committee	21 seats
Assessment Committee	12 seats
Boarding Out Committee	9 seats
Farm Committee	9 seats
Workhouse Repairs Committee	6 seats
Vagrancy Committee	3 seats

Source: CG 16 May, 1919

The power to determine the fate or fortune of the poor lay with the elected Guardians, rather than the appointed staff. The whole system was time consuming and bureaucratic, with 52 members able to participate in the decision making processes. Guardians determined every individual case for poor relief. Whilst the Master and Matron ran the workhouse on a day to day basis, they had to report in detail to the Guardians for their approval or otherwise. The detailed records kept by the Master were scrutinised by the Guardians at Board meetings. There was a visiting board or rota of Guardians who would visit the workhouse at liberty to check and report back on its condition, the state of the inmates, and the practices of the staff. All supplies of food and other materials for the workhouse were obtained by the invitation of tenders, and Guardians alone determined how tenders were awarded. Individual inmates had to present themselves before the Board in the event of misconduct for their punishment to be decided by Guardians.

Officers of the workhouse were totally subservient to the Guardians, who appointed and dismissed them, and determined their pay and conditions. Perhaps the attitude and philosophy of the Bodmin Union Guardians is best expressed by one William Phillips, when he became Chairman of the Board in May 1925, and in welcoming newly elected Guardians advised them that, "...They had to look after the poor old people who in their old age could not look after themselves, but they must not forget that it was the ratepayers who provided the money. They must do justice to all who came before them, and at the same time not impoverish the ratepayers" *(CG 1 May, 1925)*.

The most important person who attempted to advise the Guardians at Board meetings, and to ensure that they were acting legally in their deliberations, was the Clerk, whom they appointed and paid. During the 93 years that it existed the Bodmin Union Board was advised by 5 succeeding Clerks:

	Dates	Annual Salary
William R Hicks	May 1837 - Sept 1868	£100
Preston J Wallis	Oct 1868 - Oct 1891	£75-£90
Preston G Wallis	Nov 1891 - Sept 1896	£60-£85
John Pethybridge	Sept 1896 - March 1927	£80-£135
E W Gill	April 1927 - March 1930	£100

Sources: MH/9/3; and CG 7 Jan., 1927

As reflected in the salary for the post, the Clerk was the most important appointed member of staff in the local administration of the poor law system. As well as advising the Guardians in their deliberations, he had to arrange for formal minutes to be kept of all meetings, and conduct all correspondence giving effect to their decisions. A legal training was a normal requirement, although this was not the background of Bodmin Union's first Clerk.

William Robert Hicks was a schoolmaster in his early life, but devoted the majority of it subsequently to public service. As well as Clerk to the Union Board, he was for 20 years from 1840 Domestic Superintendent of the County Lunatic Asylum (calling himself 'Governor'), and Clerk to the Local Highway Board. He was elected Mayor of Bodmin in 1866, 2 years before his death, and revived at that time the ancient custom of Beating the Bounds. He was a man of wide talent, great presence, and high reputation, both locally and as far afield as London. As well as his public life, he was a musician, playing the violin to professional standard, and, above all things, a humorist and wit, being about the best local story teller of his day. He was dubbed the "Yorick of the West", a reference to a jester at Danish Court during the childhood of Shakespeare's Hamlet *(Collier, W.F.)*.

After his death in 1868, the Preston Wallis's were appointed to the Clerkship, father and son in turn, for the next 28 years. They were both solicitors and combined being Clerk to the Union Board with numerous other public positions, as well as conducting their own legal practice in the town *(Harrod's Directory, 1878, and Kelly's Directory, 1893)*. The father died in post, and the son resigned for a reason not disclosed in the surviving records *(MH/9/3)*.

John Pethybridge was Clerk to the Board for the longest period - just over 30 years from 1896 to 1927. Appointed at the age of 34 years, his service to the Board followed that of his father who had been treasurer to the first Board in 1837 *(MH/12/1294)*. Again, he combined the work with his own legal practice, and was also Clerk to the Bodmin Rural District Council during this period *(MH/9/3 and Kelly's Directory, 1893)*.

After his retirement in 1927, E W Gill, another local solicitor with his own legal firm in the town, was appointed for the final 3 years that the Board existed, until it passed into history in March, 1930 *(CG 1 April, 1927 and Kelly's Directory, 1930)*.

One of the principal measures used to gauge the success or otherwise of Guardians in dealing with the poor in their Union was that of cost to the ratepayer.

Statistics for the half year ending Michaelmas 1848 show:

Total amount of outdoor relief	£1816	6s	2d
Total amount of indoor maintenance	£ 606	0s	3½d
Maintenance of workhouse, salaries, common charges	£ 470	19s	8½d
Total cost of indoor relief at workhouse	£1077	0s	0d

Source: MH/12/1276

Assuming similar figures for the other half of the year, the total cost of indoor relief for the whole year at this time was in the order of £2154.

Almost 60 years later in 1908 the Clerk, John Pethybridge produced similar figures for the Guardians' information:

Total amount of outdoor relief	£2651	0s	0d
Total amount of indoor maintenance	£1069	12s	9d
Maintenance of workhouse, salaries, common charges	£ 947	7s	4d
Total cost of indoor relief at workhouse	£2017	0s	1d

Source: CG 9 Oct., 1908

Whilst these two annual expenditure figures are roughly the same over the 60 year period, the occupancy figures for inmates suggest a significant reduction in numbers being accommodated in the workhouse in 1908, around 100 at any one time, compared with 1848, around 140 at any one time.

The cost of indoor relief per head was always much higher than that of outdoor relief. Keeping the poor out of the workhouse and giving them modest weekly payments was much more economical and attractive to Guardians. This is reflected in both the numbers receiving the two types of relief, and the relative costs per head. In October 1904 details reported in the local newspaper from the Master's Journal recorded 77 inmates in the workhouse, and 477 persons receiving a total of £53 17s 0d in out relief. Translating the costs into the cost per head of population in the Union, indoor paupers were costing 10s 7d, compared to only 3s 9d for outdoor paupers *(CG 14 Oct., 1904)*.

In terms of comparing Bodmin workhouse with those elsewhere, figures which are available suggest that it was one of those with lower costs than the average. In 1920 figures reported to the Guardians by Ministry of Health Inspector, Mr E D Court, on one of his visits, gave the average cost per head per week for the upkeep of inmates in workhouses in the western district as 15s 2d - the cost in the Bodmin workhouse was just under 12s 0d per head *(CG 16 July, 1920)*. In January 1924, the cost for Bodmin had fallen to 7s 6¾d per head, and there were only two other Unions in the whole of the south west where lower figures were recorded *(CG 25 Jan., 1924)*. In May 1930, weekly maintenance figures per head for workhouses in Cornwall again confirm the position of Bodmin. These figures excluded establishment charges, but covered the provision of clothing and necessities, heating, lighting, surgical and medical appliances:

Camelford	12s 9½d		Launceston	8s 6¾
Truro	11s 6d		Bodmin	8s 6¾d
Liskeard	8s 8¼d		St Austell	7s 9¼d

Source: CG 22 May, 1930

As well as containing costs in the workhouse, Bodmin Guardians also appear to have been successful in dealing overall with pauperism in the Union. When Inspector Preston Thomas paid his farewell visit to Bodmin in March, 1908, he praised the Guardians for their work. The Union was one of the healthiest places and contained almost the largest proportion of old people in the West of England Unions. On the other hand, the rate of pauperism was one of the lowest and they looked after relief cases well *(CG 13 March, 1908)*. In June, 1908, in his final report to the South West Poor Law Conference, he reported that, of the 47 Unions in the western district, Bodmin was bracketed 9th lowest with Wells, recording a rate of pauperism of 30 paupers per 1000 head of population *(CG 19 June, 1908)*.

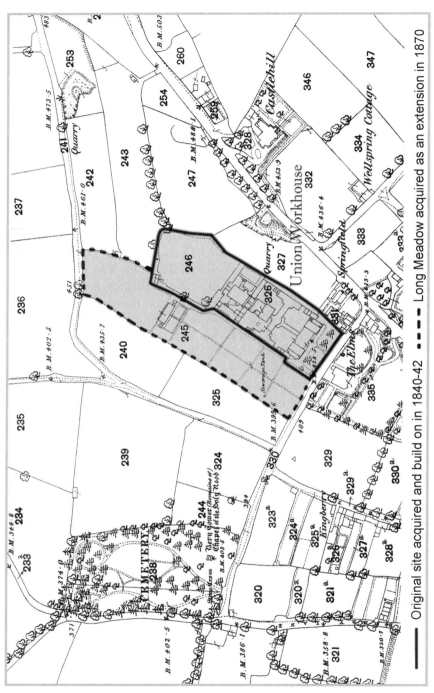

Map 2: Detailed location and boundaries of the Bodmin Union Workhouse buildings.

(Adapted from 1880, 25" to 1 mile, Ordnance Survey Map)

— Original site acquired and build on in 1840-42   • • • • Long Meadow acquired as an extension in 1870

Chapter 6

The Buildings

The comprehensiveness of the 1834 Poor Law Amendment Act for a new system to deal with the poor, extended to the design of the workhouse buildings in which those who met "the workhouse test" were to be housed. The Poor Law Commissioners emphasised that each Board of Guardians must decide themselves on the type of workhouse building which they required - although every workhouse plan had to be submitted to the Commission for final approval. To assist Guardians the Commissioners published a set of model plans in an appendix to their First Annual Report in 1835 - "We have found it necessary, for the purposes of the Act, to obtain, with professional aid, plans for the construction of workhouses of different sizes, capable of holding from one to five hundred paupers ... believing that deviations from them might be necessary to meet local circumstances" *(H M Poor Law Commissioners)*. The Commissioners further stressed that model plans were intended as a guide only - "We have therefore left to the Boards of Guardians the adoption of these, or the preference of any other plan, which contain the requisite provisions for classification of the workhouse inmates" *(H M Poor Law Commissioners)*.

The original intentions of the Commissioners were that inmates would be both classified by category, and then housed in totally separate buildings. However, this concept proved far too expensive and difficult to administer in practice. The greatest number of workhouses by far were therefore designed as "mixed", with varying degrees of internal separation for different types of inmates *(May, T)*.

The model plans produced by the Commissioners were of four main types of buildings, with two architects Sir Francis Head and Sampson Kempthorne responsible for devising them. Head devised the first plan, Kempthorne the other three. It was the plans by Kempthorne on which most of the workhouses of the 1830s and 1840s were based. His two plans, the cruciform plan and the Y plan, but particularly the cruciform version, were the model plans most frequently adopted by Guardians *(Dickens, A)*.

In both models the master's accommodation was in the centre core of the main building, with wings radiating from it. The latter contained on different floors dayrooms, sleeping accommodation, and dining halls. An entrance block housed the waiting hall with the Guardians boardroom above. A single storey range of buildings enclosed the main building, providing receiving wards and their ancillaries; refractory wards for solitary confinement; "dead houses" and workrooms.

The idea of a central core building for observation and control by the Master was based, it is suggested, on the "Panopticon principle." The Panopticon had been devised in 1787 by Jeremy Bentham, based in turn on a project by his engineer brother in Russia for a central manufacturing building controlled from a central core. Bentham considered the principle applicable to the design of prisons, primarily, but it was also adoptable he thought for lunatic asylums, poor houses, orphanages, hospitals, and many other purposes.

An important assistant to Sampson Kempthorne, as he was commissioned by Guardians to adapt his plans for them, was George Gilbert Scott, the architect who subsequently designed St Pancras station in London. Soon Scott had built up his own workhouse practice, and after leaving Kempthorne employed his own assistant, William Bonython Moffatt - a builder of Cornish origins. Over the first 10 years over 50 workhouses were erected by the Scott-Moffatt practice, after they had successfully won the competitions organised by many Union Boards to chose a design and architect for their workhouse.

Scott's earliest designs were based on the original model plans produced by Kempthorne. However, he subsequently produced a modified and slightly more humanised version of the cruciform plan, which he termed "Elizabethan", or Tudor style. His main change was to give access to the main building through a central archway in the long, low, front building, leading into an inner court, from which the entrance doors were reached. This approach to the workhouse not only gave it a more human and domestic feel, but it enabled the Master to see the porter, and the incoming paupers from his quarters in the central "octagon". *Plan 1* is a simplified version of Scott's plan.

Scott's designs and buildings extended from Lincolnshire to Cornwall, with at least a third of his output still in existence today. Typical groups of them, built between 1835 and 1840, survive in Devon and Somerset, as at Tavistock and Tiverton.

Some Guardians did not employ architects but tried their own hands at the job. Poorer Unions used the services of a local builder - the result was likely to be a plain rectangular building of local materials, surrounded on all sides by exercise yards, and with the inevitable vegetable garden at the rear. The majority of Boards of Guardians, however, put their building out to competition, or employed an acknowledged workhouse architect *(Dickens, A)*.

At their first meeting on 13 May, 1837 the Bodmin Union Board resolved that "...a workhouse be built in or near Bodmin, and that a Committee be formed for obtaining a site for the erection of a new building, and for ascertaining the capabilities of the present house for temporary purposes" *(MH/12/1274)*. It appears from the records which exist that matters must have moved quickly, because at the next meeting on 19 May, 1837 the Board resolved that "...the Workhouse Committee be requested to treat with a Mr Basset for the

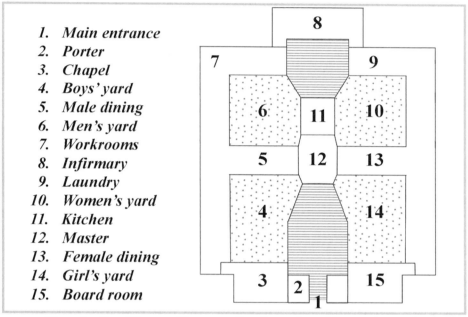

1. *Main entrance*
2. *Porter*
3. *Chapel*
4. *Boys' yard*
5. *Male dining*
6. *Men's yard*
7. *Workrooms*
8. *Infirmary*
9. *Laundry*
10. *Women's yard*
11. *Kitchen*
12. *Master*
13. *Female dining*
14. *Girl's yard*
15. *Board room*

Plan 1: Scott's workhouse plan based on Kempthorne's cruciform plan. *(Adapted from a diagram in Dickens,A)*

purchase of 2.5 acres of the field recommended as the site for the new workhouse; and to make arrangements with the Select Vestry Committee for the temporary hiring of the present workhouse" *(MH/12/1274)*.

The field chosen was known as "Baker's Field" *(PU/BOD/1)*, and was just a short distance along the lane from the Berry (see *Map 1* on page 18) - a high point on the northern side of Bodmin which appears to have had a long history, and may have been the site where the original settlement of Bodmin stood before it moved into the valley below *(Long, L.E.)*. Unfortunately, surviving records give no details of the reasons for the choice of this site for the new workhouse, but its purchase cost the Board £450 *(MH/12/1275)*.

The plans for the new workhouse are lost, and there are no details in the surviving records regarding its design and building, apart from payments being made to an architect, and a clerk of works. Unlike a number of the other Cornish Unions who engaged the London practice of Scott and Moffat to design their workhouses, Bodmin Union appears to have attempted cost savings by employing a local architect and builder. In February, 1838 the Union advertised for architects to submit their plans and terms.

The response to this newspaper advertisement is not known but within four months a further advertisement was placed in the Royal Cornwall Gazette for builders to tender to build the workhouse, based on the plans of the architect, a Mr Dwelley, Clarence Street, Plymouth.

A delay seems to have occurred after this whilst plans were finalised and authority was obtained from the Poor Law Commissioners.

In April, 1839 the Poor Law Commissioners passed an Order empowering the Bodmin Union to borrow the sum of £6450 for the purchase of the land and the construction of a new workhouse on it *(MH/12/1274)*.

By letter dated 15 June, 1839 the Clerk, William Hicks, requested the Poor Law Commissioners to provide the names of other workhouses which could be visited by the Guardians "...to profit from the experience of other Boards, and for improving the plans of their own intended workhouse"

(MH/12/1274). The Commissioners advised that any of the workhouses in Devon and Somerset would be useful to visit, the majority of which had been designed by Scott and Moffatt. It seems likely that visits were made, as the design and layout of the building by Mr Dwelley which was shortly erected at Bodmin was based on Scott's Elizabethan workhouse design.

On 27 January, 1841 William Hicks, Clerk to the Bodmin Union, wrote to the Poor Law Commissioners with plans and specifications for the new workhouse at Bodmin requesting their approval *(MH/12/1274)*. The plans were sanctioned on 26 February, 1841, subject to 4 comments:

" 1 As most of the windows to the day rooms on the ground floor are external, contact can be made between inmates and persons sent to the house. To avoid this, it is desirable to have an enclosure to the building;

2 The girls and boys require work or day rooms besides the school room being provided. These should be built in their respective yards;

3 The entrance to the probationary wards should be made through the boys and girls wards;

4 The refractory wards (solitary wards for punishment) do not require to have windows in them. They are usually lit by fanlight or iron grating over the door."

The plans and specifications were returned to the Clerk with this reply and are no longer to be found with surviving records *(MH/12/1274)*.

Work actually commenced on the new workhouse around October/November, 1840, according to the letter of 3 October,1840 from the Clerk to the Commissioners. A further letter from the Clerk dated 27 July, 1841 stated that work on the workhouse was advanced by that date *(MH/12/1274)*.

The bulk of the construction work appears to have been completed within a period of about 2 years. The Poor Law Commissioners formally authorised the new workhouse, with a capacity for 250 inmates, on 20 November, 1842. Completion works must have continued beyond this date because on 6 July, 1843 the Clerk wrote to the Commissioners regarding the total expenditure having exceeded the original authorised £6450, and requesting authority for the additional borrowing required. The total cost of the new workhouse and the land had been £7375.

On 17 August, 1843 the details of the expenditure incurred in building the new workhouse shown on the next page were sent to the Commissioners.

Whilst the architect was apparently a Mr Dwelley of Plymouth, the builder of the workhouse cannot be established. Details of the construction, layout, and function of each part are lost. A degree of conjecture is therefore used in the following description, together with using occasional bits of information in

Sums Expended

	£	s	d
Part payment of amount of contract (£5700)	5624	0	11
Sinking a well	9	17	0
Paving stones for the yards	4	18	9
Pipes etc. to convey water to wash kitchen, steam apparatus	50	0	0
Pumps	39	10	0
Gate posts	3	7	0
Drawing contract	3	0	0
Clerk of Works on a/c	85	0	0
Architect	209	0	0
TOTAL	6028	13	8

Extra outstanding sums yet to be paid

	£	s	d
Balance on amount of contract	75	19	1
Clerk of Works	85	0	0
Extra mason's work	185	7	6
Fixtures	21	17	0
Building oven to bake bread for paupers on out relief	120	0	0
Excavation of ground	29	2	0
Granite quoins	35	0	0
Enlarging well	5	0	0
Walls around drying area	10	0	0
Lead pipes, etc.	22	15	0
Cisterns and baths	37	16	5
Carpenters extras	151	9	10
Fixtures	143	16	8
Day bill for fixtures	4	13	10
TOTAL	927	17	10

the records, and a study of the plans drawn in 1986/87 for the residential conversion scheme, to make an overall assessment of the workhouse buildings, and their original uses. It is also likely that during the course of its 94 year history various adaptations were made to the original workhouse buildings, and uses changed over time.

Map 2 (page 56) shows the location of the workhouse and its boundaries. *Plan 2* shows the site layout and probable uses of the workhouse buildings.

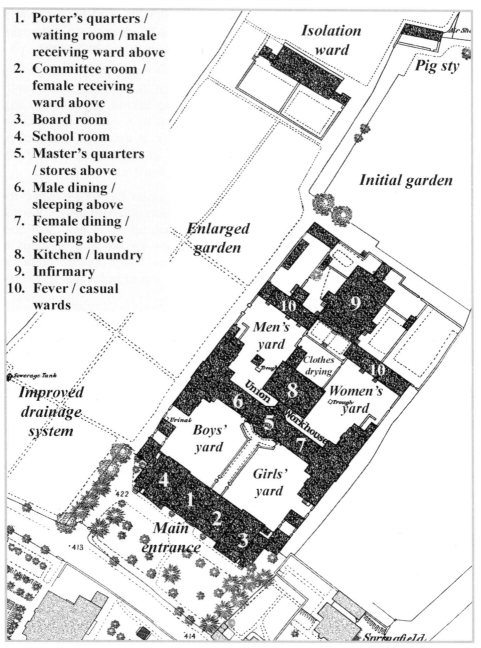

1. Porter's quarters / waiting room / male receiving ward above
2. Committee room / female receiving ward above
3. Board room
4. School room
5. Master's quarters / stores above
6. Male dining / sleeping above
7. Female dining / sleeping above
8. Kitchen / laundry
9. Infirmary
10. Fever / casual wards

Isolation ward

Pig sty

Initial garden

Enlarged garden

Improved drainage system

Sewerage Tank

Men's yard

Clothes drying

Women's yard

Union Workhouse

Boys' yard

Girls' yard

Urinal

Trough

Main entrance

Springfield

Plan 2: Detailed site layout of the Bodmin Union Workhouse.
(Adapted from 1880, 10" to 1 mile, Ordnance Survey Map)

The photographs which have been grouped together on pages 68-73 in the centre of the following detailed description of the buildings, give an impression of what they were like before and after the recent conversion took place.

As built in 1840-42 the workhouse comprised three main groups of buildings with yards between them. A low front entrance building; a main centre building with side wings and linked kitchen building behind; and a third range comprising a central infirmary fronted and flanked by single storey ancillary buildings. In plan form it bears many similarities to the Scott Elizabethan model for a workhouse layout, as found in the other Cornish workhouses which were actually designed by the Scott Moffat partnership.

All the buildings were constructed in local building stone and rubble, which the 1880 survey sheet, *Map 2* on page 56, suggests was obtained within carrying distance from a "borrow pit" or small quarry opened up in the field next door adjoining Castle Hill. This was a normal practice for erecting buildings in Bodmin as it stands on a natural bed of rock suitable for building purposes and small quarries were opened at many points in the town for building in the 19th century *(Burton, W.J.P. & Stephens, J.)*.

Distinctive architectural features on the buildings are the granite quoins on the corners, the granite kneelers at the top of the corners to support the bargeboards on the gables, and the red brick jambs and cambered heads to the windows *(English Heritage)*. On the front buildings the latter are done in yellow, rather than red bricks. The roofs were slated originally with Delabole slates. Evidence of chimney stacks, either in stone or brick, still exist at various points, and are visible in old photographs such *plate 1* (page 30).

The front entrance building

The building comprised a 2 storey centre portion, with a wing on each end, gabled front to back, and internally only one storey. In the centre at the front was a tall, wide entrance passage, with granite jambs and portal, which served as the main entrance to the centre courtyard and main centre building within. Within this entrance passage there were entrances to the right and to the left into the centre portion of the front building.

To the left, entering from the entrance passage, was probably the porters' accommodation. There are references in the records to this comprising 2 or 3 rooms in the front block *(MH/12/1275 & 1293)*. They seem to be on this side because also on this side is the original granite staircase giving access to the first floor above. One of the main duties of the porter was to receive new inmates and to hold them, whilst their futures were decided by the

Guardians. It seems possible that one of the rooms was the waiting room after initial arrival, and upstairs were the receiving wards or dormitories for sleeping, separate for men and women. An internal corridor possibly ran through the porter's quarters on the ground floor giving access to the cross gable wing.

To the right, entering from the entrance passage, there was just one large room at the front, with a corridor leading through to the cross gable wing on the other end. There was no access on this side to the first floor above, and it seems likely that this may have been the room in which the Board of Guardians held their various Committee meetings.

The main cross gable wings on each end of the front building contained single large rooms of considerable height, as there was no first floor above. The possibility is that they were the original schoolroom and Boardroom respectively. References in the records suggest that there was only one schoolroom, divided internally, if only by a curtain, between the boys and girls. The stronger presumption is that it was in the left hand wing, accessed either along the corridor through the porter's quarters, or by a rear door directly into the centre courtyard. If this presumption is correct, the Board Room where the Guardians held their fortnightly board meetings was in the other cross wing room on the right hand wing. The Board Room was usually one of the grandest in the workhouse to satisfy the self importance of Guardian Boards, and would have needed to be large to accommodate all 52 of them should a meeting be fully attended. Styles varied between workhouses but in 1865 the Social Science Review pictured the typical Board Room as "...a mixture of an Old Bailey Court, a small chapel, and a third class railway waiting room..." (May, T.).

On the sides of the main cross gable wings are smaller and lower parallel wings with gabled granite dressed porches at the front. The purpose of these buildings cannot now be determined, other than supposing that perhaps they were used ancillary to the school room and Board Room respectively.

At the back of the front building, and between the rear projections of the two end cross gable wings, was a ground floor lean-to. On the left hand side, it contained part of the porter's quarters, but on the right hand side its purpose is not clear.

The centre courtyard

The centre courtyard was divided by the walled central access way, leading from the passageway through the front building, to entrance doors each side of the centre octagon in the centre building. The 1880 plan shows a building on the left hand side marked "urinal", and on this basis the presumption is made that the boys used the left hand yard, and the girls were confined to the right hand yard.

Main centre building

The main building consists of a central range and equal side wings, all of 2 storeys, with in the centre a 3 storey block of octagonal plan and pyramidal roof - the Panopticon of Jeremy Bentham and Sampson Kempthorne to oversee the whole of the workhouse layout.

The division of this building into its separate original individual functions is impossible without the original documentation. Three presumptions are put forward based on the model plans described previously:

1   The Master and Matron and their family had their accommodation somewhere in the central core, together with the storage of the workhouse supplies close by to safeguard against theft;

2   Men and boys were accommodated in the left hand parts of the building; and women and girls in the right hand parts. This follows from the premise used previously to divide the centre courtyards with boys on the left, and girls on the right;

3   Dining rooms were on each side of the centre at ground floor level, connected with the kitchen block behind, and dormitory accommodation was provided for sleeping on the first floor above. Again men and boys eating and sleeping on the left hand side of the building, and women and girls on the right hand side.

The main entrance and exit points to the ground floor of the centre building were via the doorways each side of the central octagon, and approached from the front building by the stone walled walkway dividing the central yards. The main access to the first floor was via two granite stairways, one at each end of the central range, with doorways in each corner at the junction with the cross wings.

Details in visiting Inspectors reports towards the end of the 1880s suggest that there were separate dormitories in the main centre building for the able bodied, the old, and the children. The remainder of the centre buildings must have had rooms for various purposes, in particular day rooms for each category of inmate.

The inspection report by Local Government Board Inspector, Lord Courtenay, in December, 1895 *(MH/12/1293)* contains the following statistics on the dormitory accommodation at that time:

		Beds Provided	Beds Occupied
Men	Able bodied	16	2
	Old men	8	8
	Boys	23	15
Women	Able bodied	16	12
	Old women	16	12
	Girls	16	12

As far as the kitchen building is concerned at the rear of the centre building, there are no details available other than the photographs of the original building, and the references in the expenditure details to steam apparatus and an oven for baking bread. The photographs show a distinctive glass "hood" on the apex of the roof for securing maximum light into the working areas within. This feature caused the kitchen block to be known more recently as the "Lantern Building".

There is a presumption that it may have also originally contained the main washroom for inmates. It was the only place in the workhouse where a supply of hot and cold water was readily available for the purpose of washing. Otherwise, for probably 50 years or so, hot water had to be carried everywhere else in the workhouse from here. The washing of clothes was also probably undertaken in or outside the kitchen block. In the yards on each side of the building there was a large granite trough for this purpose.

Rear courtyard

The kitchen building and an enclosed yard at the back of it, probably a clothes drying area, effectively divided the rear courtyard into two distinct yards as in the centre courtyard - the men's yard to the left, and the women's yard to the right. In the men's yard beside their granite washing trough there was the well, dug to provide the original water supply for the workhouse.

Infirmary and ancillary buildings

This was the third major group of buildings erected as part of the original workhouse beyond the rear courtyards. Again, there are no detailed records surviving with the functions and layouts, both of which probably changed over time. The visiting Inspector's report in 1869 *(MH/12/1280)* suggests that the two single storey ancillary buildings each side of the infirmary at the front were being used at that time as detached wards for fever and other infectious diseases, as well as for other purposes, so that their effectiveness to stop the spread of these diseases was questionable - men on the left, women on the right. Subsequently, when these wards had been discontinued and replaced by an entirely separate isolation block, it seems that the two buildings were

Plate 3: Original front entrance building to the workhouse.
(Bodmin Research Project)

Plate 4: Front entrance building after conversion.

Plate 5: The front of the main central accommodation block. *(Bodmin Research Project)*

Plate 6: Markings on the slate window sills in the girls' yard.

Plate 7: Markings on the slate window sills in the boys' yard.

Plate 8: The original kitchen/laundry or 'lantern' block at the rear of the main centre building.

Plate 9: The rebuilt 'lantern' block.

Plate 10: The main infirmary building at the rear of the workhouse.

Plate 11:   The front of the original isolation ward, built in the enlarged workhouse garden.

Plate 12: The original piggery built at the top of the garden.

used as casual wards for tramps and vagrants seeking overnight accommodation at the workhouse.

For the two storey infirmary there are very limited details available. Essentially, it appears to have been divided into male and female wards, with children and adults mixed together, as well as all types of illnesses and conditions mixed together. For women there was a separate lying in ward, for pre- and post-childbirth at the workhouse. The infirmary nurse at the end of the 1800s appeared to have had no separate quarters but slept in the women's ward.

The statistics in visiting Inspector's reports give an indication of the infirmary accommodation. In March, 1869 when there was the main infirmary and the detached ancillary buildings at the front in use for fever and other infectious diseases, Inspector Lougley recorded:

	Men		**Women**		**Total**	
	Wards	Beds	Wards	Beds	Wards	Beds
Ordinary	1	7	2	14	3	21
Fever/smallpox	1	5	1	3	2	8
Venereal	-	-	1	3	1	3
Lying in	-	-	1	3	1	3
				Total	7	35

Source: MH/12/1280

In April, 1897, after the ancillary buildings had been discontinued and a separate isolation block for infectious diseases had been built, Inspector Preston Thomas recorded:

		Beds Provided	**Beds Occupied**
Men	Infirmary	12	6
	Infectious	4	-
Women	Infirmary	20	17
	Lying in	3	2
	Infectious	4	-

Source: MH/12/1295

In 1872, after pressure from both visiting Inspectors, and Guardians visiting the workhouse as the Visiting Committee for inspection, it was decided to separate infectious cases entirely from the infirmary complex by the building of an isolated infectious building. With the acquisition of Long Meadow, 2 years earlier (see below for details), there was now space for this to be possible, and a site was selected in it opposite the original workhouse garden. In July, 1872 the Clerk submitted plans to the Local Government Board for their approval. A single storey building was proposed, similar in style and materials to the original workhouse, with accommodation for 4 patients of each sex in separate wards. The cost was estimated at £375 for the building, and the project received approval to proceed in December, 1872. Building works commenced in 1873, and by the end of the year the infectious wards were nearing completion *(MH/12/1281)*.

Workhouse Gardens

The original workhouse garden was above the infirmary building, with, in the top corner, a small stone building used for the keeping of pigs.

In 1870 the Guardians sought to enlarge the workhouse garden by purchasing the adjoining field, about 3 acres in size, to the west of Ennis Lane, known as Long Meadow and owned by a Peter Hoblyn. This was considered desirable so that a larger quantity of potatoes could be grown, "..which are now a serious item of expenditure." The purchase duly took place for the sum of £400 *(MH/12/1280)*.

Services to the workhouse

It was not until the end of the 1800s and early 1900s that the links were made between personal health and such public health matters as satisfactory foul drainage, and a wholesome water supply.

In 1869 the visiting Poor Law Board Inspector commented on "...the most offensive cesspools in the immediate vicinity of the house which could account for the outburst of fever..." He recommended that without delay alterations should be made to these cesspits *(MH/12/1280)*.

In September, 1880, some 11 years later, a successor Inspector was able to report that the foul drainage had now been put in order and was carried to a main drain *(MH/12/1284)*. It appears that the purchase of Long Meadow in 1870 had allowed the drainage arrangements to be improved. The 1880 Ordnance Survey plan, *Plan 2* on page 63, indicates a sewerage tank in that part of it being used by then as the enlarged workhouse garden *(MH/12/1284)*. There is also a record in January, 1879 that a notice was served on the Guardians by Bodmin Sanitary Authority requiring the Board to connect the workhouse to the new main sewer of the Borough - dramatic improvements had been carried out during the 1870s to eliminate the foul smelling pool of town sewage which previously had existed in the vicinity of the prison.

Whilst mains drainage to the workhouse appears to have been provided by the 1880s, sanitary conditions within it remained primitive. In April 1897 Inspector Preston Thomas reported that earth closets were still in use, with only slop and other waste water going into the town sewer *(MH/12/1295)*. It was not until August, 1901 that the Board's House Committee recommended that the outdoor earth closets should be discontinued, and specifications were prepared for fitting 2 indoor water closets *(CG 23 Aug.,1901)*.

A better quality water supply to replace the workhouse well water came later than the town sewer. In June, 1895 the Board entered into an agreement with the Bodmin Water Company for a continuous supply of water *(MH/12/1293)*. It was also agreed at this time to erect water hydrants in several places for fire fighting purposes. By 1897 Preston Thomas reported that "...the town's supply of main water to the workhouse was unlimited..." *(MH/12/1295)*.

As far as the other basic facilities of heating and lighting were concerned, they were probably little different from most working class households outside the workhouse. The only heating was from coal fires in some of the rooms - otherwise there was none. Photographs of the old buildings as on page 30 indicate a number of chimney stacks, and capped stacks are still visible on some of the external walls of the buildings today. Lighting was by candle and paraffin oil lamp, until 1908 when the Board agreed to the first installation of gas for some lighting and other purposes, based on a specification from the Bodmin Gas Company *(CG 9 Oct., 1908)*. The telephone was connected in 1914 at a cost of £6 per year as it was considered expedient in the event of fire and for the calling of the doctor *(CG 6 Feb., 1914)*. Electricity for more general lighting in the workhouse did not take place until the 1920s *(CG 30 Jan, 1920)*.

The workhouse name

Finally, the name of the workhouse changed during its 94 years to reflect the changing attitudes towards the plight of the poor during this period. From 1842-1904 it was referred to simply as the Bodmin Union Workhouse, the mere mention of the name intended to strike fear and shame into the working class. At the end of 1904 it was decided nationally to reduce the stigma of workhouses by inviting Unions to call their workhouses by a private name. The Local Government Board sanctioned an initiative from the Registrar General that in future all details recording the birth of children in Poor Law institutions should not include any direct reference to the workhouse *(PU/BOD/7)*. In November, 1904 the Bodmin Guardians decided that the Bodmin Union Workhouse would be known from 1 January 1905 as Berry Tower House *(CG 25 Nov., 1904)*. This name remained until it was national dictat to change again and it was decreed that all workhouses should be known simply as Institutions. Bodmin Union or Berry Tower Institution remained the name until its demise, although the stigma of the workhouse remained even if the term "workhouse" had been long abandoned.

Chapter 7

Life And Times In The Workhouse

The Main House

Three smells immediately struck visitors to workhouses in the 19th century - whitewash, overcooked cabbage, and urine! *(Crowther, M.A.)* Sensations prompted by the copious application of whitewash as the easiest and cleanest form of internal decoration everywhere; the poor standard of food, and more significantly its cooking by untrained paupers in the kitchens; and the poor standards of hygiene and sanitation.

In a word, conditions were austere. Inmates had all their possessions removed from them on entry, as well as their personal freedom and liberty before they left again. Daily life was governed by regulations which were strictly enforced. The whole intent of the 1834 Act was to punish inmates for landing themselves in the workhouse and having to be supported by common funds. Dehumanising the individual was considered to be the key to making those within the system strive harder to make a better life, as well as warning those without the workhouse walls what would be their fate if they thought poor relief was an easy option.

The workhouse day was long and tedious. It was ordered according to central regulations. The detailed timetable within Bodmin Union workhouse is not available, but one may suppose that it was based fairly closely on the Commissioners Model Timetable. This recommended that the workhouse bell should ring at 5am from March to September, and at 7am for the rest of the year; breakfast, preceded by prayers, followed from 6-7 (7.30 or 8 in winter) and then work from 7 (8 in winter) until 12; 12-1 for dinner; 1-6 work again; 6-7 supper; followed by more prayers, then bed by 8 at latest *(Longmate, N.)*.

The length of time for meal breaks gives a false impression that workhouse fare was to be enjoyed. Quite the reverse. The food was intended to be as dull, predictable, and tasteless as possible. Again, until 1900 its amount and content was strictly controlled by central regulation, based on one of the 6 Model Diets recommended by the Commission *(Longmate, N.)*.

At the opening of Bodmin workhouse in 1842 the dietary approved, after criticism and amendment by the Commissioners, comprised the following:

Breakfast:	Daily:	7oz bread, 1.5pts milk broth
Dinner:	Sat:	1½lbs stew containing 1½oz of meat
	Sun:	4oz cooked meat, 1lb potato or other veg
	Mon:	1¼lbs potato or other veg, 2 pilchards or herrings
	Tue:	1½lbs stew
	Wed:	1½pts pea soup, 1oz bacon, 4oz bread
	Thu:	1lb 13oz stew, with 1oz bacon and pudding covering
	Fri:	1½pts rice milk, 5oz bread
Supper:	Mon-Sat:	7oz bread, 1½pts milk broth
	Sunday:	7oz bread, 1½pts meat broth

Source: MH/12/1274

Women had the same diet as men, apart from those meals where bread was provided - in the case of bread they always had 1oz less!

For children above 9 years old the diet was the same as the above - below the age of 9 there was discretion to vary it.

For inmates above the age of 60 years, there was an allowance of 1oz tea, 4oz butter, and 4oz sugar in lieu of the milk broth.

For the sick in the infirmary, the dietary could be varied at the discretion of the Medical Officer.

The workhouse dietary approved initially in 1843 was revised a number of times as the 1800s progressed, subject to central approval on each occasion. In December 1869, 4 revised dietaries were approved, respectively for the able bodied paupers; for the aged, infirm and imbeciles; for children 2-5 years old; and for children 5-9 years old. The details contain interesting lists of the prescribed mix of ingredients which had to be used in some of the main dishes:

Pea Soup - each gallon had to contain
    32oz of shins of beef
    1pt of split peas
    8oz of carrots, onions, turnips, or leeks

Irish Stew - each 24oz had to contain
    4oz of meat
    10oz of potatoes
    2oz of carrots, onions, turnips, etc.

Milk Broth - each gallon had to contain
    5oz of oatmeal
    2pts of milk

Source: MH/12/1280

The dietary ingredients were supplied to the kitchen either from the workhouse garden, or by outside suppliers. In the case of outside suppliers, business with them was always conducted on a tendering basis. The Master was responsible for organising this and for keeping the detailed records on quantities and payments. Bureaucracy ruled the procurement of supplies and their use within the workhouse - even down to accounting for amounts of food wasted so that totals consumed, equated with totals of raw materials supplied. The detailed records kept by the Master were scrutinised by the central auditors once or twice a year, as well as being reported to and scrutinised by the Guardians at their fortnightly Board meetings.

The advertisement placed in the Royal Cornwall Gazette in February, 1840, and reproduced on the following page, indicates the supplies for which tenders were being invited at that time, and gives other insights into how life must have been in the temporary workhouse whilst the new one was being erected.

At the Board meeting on 9 November, 1878 the record of invoices paid over the previous 2 weeks shows details of local suppliers from the town, as well as amounts being spent:

Provisions	Heygate - grocer	£ 1	19s	8d
	Cardell - grocer		16s	11d
	Pascoe - miller	£ 8	5s	10½d
	Spear - butcher	£ 7	18s	4d
	Perry - dairyman	£ 1	16s	7d
	Total	£20	17s	4½d

Source: PU/BOD/2

Details of the work regime for inmates are not available from surviving records, but inferences suggest that most of the regime revolved around the domestic routines and upkeep of the workhouse. With the limited staff resources, pauper labour was essential to run a household which could number upwards of 150 in total at times. Kitchen duties no doubt kept many busy, under the supervision of the Matron, as well as general cleaning and scrubbing throughout. Prior to the end of the 1800s the workhouse infirmary functioned largely with pauper labour, supervised again by the Matron. The workhouse garden kept some of the men and older boys busy. Day rooms and work rooms existed, but the activities carried on in them are not clear.

The children spent much of the day in the school room, or in the day rooms, in theory at least under the charge of the schoolmistress and master. However, the use of pauper labour, and the fact that strict segregation of the different categories of inmate was virtually impossible in such a small workhouse as

BODMIN UNION.

[DUTY FREE.]

To Drapers, Bakers, Butchers, Millers, Grocers, Shoemakers, and Others.

PERSONS desirous of Contracting with the Board of Guardians of this Union, for supplying them with all or any of the undermentioned Articles, at such times and places, and in such quantities, as the Board may direct, for Twelve Months, from the 21st of March next, (except the Bread, which is to be supplied for Three Months only,) are requested to send Sealed Tenders, free of expense, to my Office in Bodmin addressed "*To the Clerk of the Guardians of the Bodmin Union,*" with the nature of the Tender endorsed thereon, on or before FRIDAY, the 7th of March.

Best Seconds Bread, in Loaves of 4lbs. each, for the Workhouse, and for all or any of the Parishes in the Union, at per loaf.

Beef, to consist of Shins, Rounds, Butts, & Flanks, at per lb.

Suet, at per lb.

Mutton, describing the Joint or Piece, at per lb.

Bacon, at per lb.

Fresh Butter, to be delivered weekly, at per lb.

Salt Butter, at per lb.

Potatoes, varying with the seasons at per bag of 7 score.

Boiling Peas, at per bushel.

Oatmeal, at per cwt.

Salt, at per cwt.

Soap, (best yellow,) at per doz. lb.

Candles, moulds, dip, and rush, at per doz. lb.

Rice, at per cwt.

Treacle, at per lb.

Good Congou Tea and Sugar, at per lb.

Scalded or Skimmed Milk, to be delivered daily, at per gal.

Brooms and Brushes, at per doz.

Coals, (best Newport,) at per ton.

Fagot Wood and Furze, at per hundred.

Flour, (best Seconds,) at per sack of 14 score.

Men's and Boys' Hats, each.

Caps for Boys, each.

Women's and Girls' Straw Bonnets, each.

Stout blue printed Cottons for Gowns, at per yard.

Hessians, at per yard.

Calico, stout and plain, at per yard.

Twilled Cotton, (white and coloured,) at per yard.

Serge, at per yard.

Flannel, at per yard.

Dark Speckled, and black Worsted, at per lb.

Men's, Youths', and Boys' Suits of strong grey Cloth, at per suit.

Ditto, ditto, of Fustina, at per suit.

Strong Cotton Counterpanes, coloured, each.

Sheets, stout brown cotton, at per pair.

Blankets, stout, at per pair.

Sheetings, stout brown, at per yard.

Coverlids, at per doz.

Bed Ticking, at per yard.

Check, at per yard.

Men's and Boys' strong Shoes, nailed & ironed, at per pair.

Women's and Girls' Shoes, at per pair.

The whole of the Articles must be of good quality, delivered free of expense, and subject to the approval of the Board of Guardians, or their Officers; and the Party contracting must, if required, give security for the specific performance of the contract.

Further particulars may be obtained on personal application.

W. R. HICKS, Clerk, &c.

Bodmin, February 25, 1840.

Royal Cornwall Gazette

Bodmin, inevitably led to children and adults mixing. In 1847 Inspector Gulson expressed his concern to the Guardians that "...girls and women in the nursery are using the same privy during school hours, and several of these women are of immoral habit..."*(MH/12/1275)*. He recommended that the arrangement was most objectionable and the two should not communicate. The Clerk subsequently wrote to the Commissioners confirming that "...steps will be taken to prevent women from having access to the girl's yard..." *(MH/12/1275)*. In 1856 the same Inspector criticised the schoolmaster, Richard Lawry, for allowing some of the boys to mix with the men, and not looking after them sufficiently after school hours *(MH/12/1277)*. In 1870 one of the Union School Inspectors, Mr T B Browne, criticised the Guardians for allowing girls to wash under the charge of an adult female inmate who was the mother of two illegitimate children. Again, the Guardians acted and subsequently discontinued the practice *(MH/12/1280)*.

With the children, the main aim of the Guardians was to get them out of the workhouse and into employment, where they could be self supporting, as soon as possible. Maybe at times they were a little over anxious in this. In 1872 the Guardians were advised that it was not desirable to send children out to employment under 12 years of age *(MH/12/1281)*. The local newspaper records in May, 1901 that children were sent out to local service, boys to farms in the area, and girls into domestic service. The arrangements regarding wages, clothes, and pocket money in each case were determined by the Guardians on their merits *(CG 31 May, 1901)*.

Within the workhouse it is probably a mistaken impression that the work periods were busy and productive for everyone. Time no doubt dragged for many due to under occupation and lack of purpose. Idle hands and rebelliousness could lead to discipline and punishment. At the meeting of the Board on 26 October, 1878 three pauper inmates in the workhouse, Hancock, Duslow, and Pearse, were summoned to appear before the Board, charged by the Master with having appropriated for their own use some flour, suet, and meat whilst being employed in the kitchen. They admitted their guilt, and the Master was instructed to keep them in solitary confinement on bread and water for 24 hours, before removing them from the kitchen and placing them at the hardest work in the workhouse *(PU/BOD/2)*.

On 6 October, 1898 Board Members were surprised to learn of a windowless room in the workhouse used for punishment purposes. The Chairman of the House Committee thought the existence of such a room acted as a deterrent without it actually being used, but reference to the Master's punishment book revealed that occasionally inmates were given periods of incarceration in it *(Barton, R.M.)*.

During the 1800s the health of those in the main house varied according to the time of year, and whether or not the house was in the grip of any fever epidemic. Scarlet fever was particularly common, with typhoid fever and smallpox other possibilities. The Poor Law Inspector visiting in 1869 found "..a great deal of fever in the house, with no means of separating fever cases from the general sick. Measles had broken out amongst the workhouse children, with 18 boys and 15 girls affected..." (MH/12/1280). In 1879 the Medical Officer reported by letter to the Board that the Master was suffering from a modified attack of typhoid fever, and there were also several cases of scarlet fever in the house. They had been sent to the recently erected isolation ward for infectious cases at the top of the workhouse garden, and every attempt was being made to halt the spread of the disease. After some 3 weeks in the isolation ward the Medical Officer was able to report that the children were much better and would be brought down into the body of the workhouse again shortly (PU/BOD/2).

Washing, bathing, and standards of personal hygiene clearly left much to be desired according to Inspectors' reports during the 1800s, and even into the early 1900s. In December, 1895 the Local Government Board requested the Bodmin Union to improve the supply of hot water to the workhouse (MH/12/1293). The Inspector's subsequent report in October, 1896 notes that "...There is no change in the workhouse since my last visit, the Guardians having taken no notice of my suggestions in the Visiting Committee Book, nor the Board's letter with regard to hot water supply and bathing accommodation..." (MH/12/1294). This remained the situation the following year when the Inspector noted that as far as the children were concerned "...their condition is not altogether satisfactory and there is no bathing accommodation for them..." (MH/12/1295). Whilst improvements followed they clearly took time. In 1912 Inspector Court issued a critical report on the workhouse to Guardians, and amongst other things noted that "...bathing arrangements for men need improving..." (CG 23 Feb., 1912). This same matter was still concerning the Ministry of Health Inspector in 1924 when he suggested that "...hot water apparatus be installed in connection with the bath on the male side of the house, as at present only cold water is laid on and hot water has to be carried a considerable distance..." (CG 11 Jan., 1924).

Nevertheless, despite these shortcomings in workhouse conditions and comforts, improvements had occurred by the end of the 1800s. Some of these chief reforms were in the province of public health, and the recognition that hygiene was a crucial factor in the prevention of disease. As Preston Thomas notes "..diseases which declined fastest were those chiefly influenced by sanitary conditions. Typhoid fever was a typical example, with mortality being reduced by some 75%..." *(Preston-Thomas, H.)*. The health of the main house at Bodmin workhouse appears to have improved significantly by the beginning of the 1900s, undoubtedly as a result of the isolation wards built in 1873 to remove infectious cases from both the main house and the infirmary, the improved drainage arrangements carried out during the 1870s, and the town water supply introduced into the workhouse in the 1890s.

The conditions for children in workhouses generally were open to criticism by the end of the 19th century. Workhouse schools had started being abolished in the 1870s, but it was 1895 before the Bodmin Union schoolhouse was closed *(MH/12/1293)*. For the first time children could escape the continuous confines of the workhouse, and could mix with other children and teachers outside. However, this was only the first step, and the ultimate solution was to have them removed from the workhouse altogether. In the Bodmin workhouse this did not happen until 1913 for girls, and 1915 for boys.

In the meantime, conditions in the main house for children were criticised by successive Inspectors. Inspector Andrew Fuller in December,1897 noted that, for the limited size of Bodmin workhouse, there was an unduly large number of children in it. He observed that some of their boots were too small for their feet, and recommended that in addition to better fitting boots, it would be to their advantage if they were provided with slippers to wear in the house *(MH/12/1295)*.

The sleeping arrangements for children had been criticised as early as 1856 by Inspector Gulson who noted that the regulations regarding the sleeping of children in the workhouse were neglected, with 3 girls in each bed of different ages *(MH/12/1277)*. In 1912, almost 60 years later, Inspector Court was commenting that "...there is still a need for more beds in the children's rooms to avoid the placing of 2 or more in a bed..." He also suggested that more use should be made in the evenings of the children's meal room for one sex, rather than placing boys, girls, and infants into the one rough day room *(CG 23 Feb., 1912)*.

One highlight in the year to break the monotony of the daily routines was Christmas. Even in 1843 the Guardians resolved that the paupers should have roast beef and plum pudding for dinner on Christmas Day *(PU/BOD/1)*. This practice continued through the 1800s, and in the early 1900s, with central controls over the Guardians being relaxed, Christmas festivities in the workhouse became a grander affair. The local Cornish Guardian newspaper on 2 January, 1903 recorded this account of "Christmas at Bodmin Union - A Splendid Bill of Fare":

In accordance with the long established custom, the inmates of this institution have again been provided with their festive fare, commencing with tea on Christmas Eve, and roast beef and plum pudding for their dinner on Christmas Day, at which latter event the Guardians in the immediate neighbourhood generally make a point of attending. It might interest many of our readers to know that the late Alderman Thomas Baron for a number of years used to attend and assist at the dinner on Christmas Day, and made various gifts to the old and young people. Since his decease, however, his daughters the Misses E and F Baron, of the Mayoralty, have been very good in continuing this act of kindness, which the inmates look forward to with no small amount of pleasure. At the dinner on Christmas Day this year the Guardians in attendance were Messrs G C Carpenter, Julian Glanville and W Martyn, whilst Miss E Baron attended and afterwards made gifts of sweets, oranges, and nuts to the children and grown-ups, a present of money to the old men, and tea to the women. Messrs Glanville and Martyn wished all a merry Christmas and a happy New Year on behalf of the Guardians, and expressed themselves pleased at having seen them enjoy their dinner so thoroughly.

On Monday evening through the kindness of Miss Guy (one of the lady Guardians) the inmates were given oranges and hot pasties; those in the body of the house congregating in the kitchens where songs were sung; whilst the patients in the hospital were visited by Miss Guy who made the gifts personally throughout.

On Tuesday evening the annual tea, which is provided through the generosity of the Guardians and a few friends took place, and ample justice was apparently done. At the conclusion of the tea a concert, which had been arranged for in the Board room was patronised by those who could attend from the House and several from outside, who included Miss Guy, Messrs G C Carpenter, and W Fish (Guardians), and Mr John Pethybridge (Clerk) and Mrs Pethybridge. The programme, as usual, was of a most entertaining description, and special thanks are due to everybody who took part in or helped in any way to effect such a pleasant evening. Mr John Wood came purposely from Lostwithiel to give a repetition of his successful gramophone entertainment of a few weeks since, and although his machine was evidently somewhat affected by the damp weather, still a performance was sufficient to win hearty applause. Mr W G Tickell again carried out the comical element in an excellent manner. He sang "All he said was 'Ha! ha! ha!'", "Stammering sweethearts", and "Gallery and boxes", of course receiving encores to each, to which he responded with "All of a sudden he stopped", "Close", and "Three nice girls". It is believed Mr Tickell has never before so aroused the mirth of an audience - in fact, it was a difficult matter to keep under subjection during any portion of his songs, as they were sung in such comic vein. Mr Tickell certainly eclipsed himself on this occasion. Mr T B Mallins recited in his usual irreproachable style "Billy Shaw", a tale of the village oracle's explanation of the difference between a play and an opera; which needless to say was of a most educating character! Mr E Johns, assisting on the spur of the moment, gave a recitation entitled "Kissing Cup", which was fully appreciated and given hearty applause. Mr Fred Climo sang "Nazareth" and the "Skipper of St Ives" (by request) receiving an encore for the latter, and responding with "The Old Brigade".

At the conclusion of the programme, Mr Pethybridge proposed a hearty vote of thanks to all who had taken part, to which Mr G C Carpenter added his testimony by seconding, and which was carried unanimously, thus giving a fitting termination to a very successful entertainment. The accompaniments were efficiently provided by Miss E Bennett and Mr Tom Whale on the piano kindly lent by Mr S Tickell. The dining room was prettily decorated by the officers.

This account of Christmas in 1903 reflects the increasing concern of the Guardians in the 20th century to improve the comforts for the inmates, both in the main house and in the infirmary. This they were enabled to do by the various changes in the regulations which occurred at the beginning of the century, lessening central controls and giving them greater freedom locally over how they ran their own Union and workhouse.

Entertainment for the inmates started to be provided on occasions other than Christmas. In November, 1901 it was agreed by the Guardians that the Bodmin Concert Party would give a series of winter concerts in the workhouse *(CG 1 Nov., 1901)*. In September, 1922 the House Committee considered arrangements for the entertainment of the inmates during the winter months. The Committee recommended that the Guardians from Bodmin Borough should form a Committee to make appropriate arrangements. There were several musically inclined people in Bodmin who were willing to assist in brightening the lives of inmates *(CG 22 Sept., 1922)*. In 1923 a piano was presented to the house for the use of inmates at the various entertainments held during the year. It had cost £40 and was paid for largely by subscriptions given by the 52 Guardians on the Union Board. The old harmonium, already in the house, was moved into the infirmary for the entertainment there of the old who were too weak to come into the main house *(CG 23 March, 1923)*.

Christmas celebrations always remained the highlight of the year. At Christmas 1920 the Mayor of Bodmin, Mr H Liddell, gave 1s to each adult inmate in the house, and 6d to each of the children *(CG 31 Dec., 1920)*.

Plate 13: The Union Workhouse concert party in the 1920's pose with their matron Mrs. Benny, right, and deputy, Miss Cloak, left.
(Pat Munn Collection)

Bodmin Male Voice Choir visited the house to give entertainment to the inmates, and at the end of January, 1921 all the inmates of the workhouse and scattered homes were invited to attend a film showing at the Turrett Kinema in Bodmin *(CG 28 Jan., 1921)*. The following Christmas the Mayor and Mayoress gave all the inmates a Christmas tea and entertainment - a "Professor Johns" from Plymouth had been secured for the evening to give a performance of conjuring and shadowgraphy; several Bodmin artists had also promised to help with the musical part of the programme *(CG 5 Dec., 1921)*. The generosity of the Guardians also extended at this time of year to the provision of a special tea for inmates on New Years Day.

In the summer time of each year another event, much anticipated by inmates, was the annual outing, funded by the Guardians, to the seaside. In August, 1921, accompanied by their officials and the Chairman of the Board, Mr G C Carpenter, they went by brakes and jersey car to Porthpean. Despite the fact that it rained all day it is reported that they had an enjoyable day, and returned home without mishap *(CG 12 Aug., 1921)*. Other years Polzeath was a popular venue for the outing *(CG 25 July, 1924)*.

Special events were also celebrated by the workhouse inmates. In June,1911, to celebrate the coronation of George V, the Board agreed to give all adult inmates 1s and children 6d during Coronation week, with a special tea being provided for them on Coronation Day. The Bodmin Corporation Committee also invited the children to attend the special celebrations in the Borough *(CG 16 June, 1911)*. The end of the Great War was celebrated by the inmates holding their own Peace celebrations. Ham and eggs were served for breakfast, with dinner comprising a leg of lamb and pork, accompanied by vegetables, junket, blancmange, stewed fruit and cream *(CG 25 July, 1919)*.

Whilst these special events were exceptional, local newspaper reports suggest that conditions in the main house during the 1920s were much improved from earlier, and would have been envied by those inmates who had endured the deprivations of most of the 1800s. A more caring attitude for the poor and their plight had emerged, to replace the idea of punishing them as intended by the original 1834 Act. In October, 1925 Mr Duff, the South West Inspector of the Ministry of Health, attended the Board meeting and reported that, having been over the Children's Homes and the workhouse, he was "...pleased and impressed..." with everything that he had seen *(CG 2 Oct., 1925)*.

The Workhouse School

Conditions in the workhouse school can only be glimpsed from the few records which remain.

Soon after opening in November, 1843 there is a record of a cheque for 3s 6d being paid to the Rev C Grylls for the purchase of scripture books for use in the school. In June, 1844 the Guardians resolved to purchase slates and pencils for the school so that the children could be taught to write *(PU/BOD/1)*.

In June, 1847 on his first visit, the Assistant Poor Law Commissioner, Edward Gulson, found the school arrangements somewhat lacking. 37 boys were being taught, but without any copy books, although he was told that they had been ordered. For the 57 girls attending, there were also no copy books for writing, and even worse, none had been ordered. The only books being used appeared to be the scripture books purchased from the Rev Grylls *(MH/12/1275)*.

Whilst things improved slightly after this visit, changes for the better only occurred after continuous promptings from Inspectors following their visits. In March, 1851 a list of books and other apparatus was put forward by the school inspector as being needed in the workhouse school:

24 x 2nd reading books	8s 0d
24 x 3rd reading books	16s 0d
24 Bibles	£1 0s 0d

12 x Testaments	4s 6d
Map of Palestine	8s 0d
Map of England	8s 0d
Map of the World	10s 6d
Total	£3 15s 0d

Large blackboard 6' x 5'
Ruled copy books
Additional writing desk

Source: MH/12/1276

For the use of the teacher, the following reference books were recommended: Notes on the Gospels; Help to Catechizing; Geography of Palestine; First Principles of Arithmetic.

In 1865, the first step to accommodate and teach children outside the workhouse was taken. St Guron's Home and Industrial School was established to accommodate 14 girls. About half this number was recommended by the Guardians from the workhouse and paid for from the poor law rates. An allowance of 2s. a week each was paid until girls reached the age of 13 years when they were placed in domestic service outside the home *(Kelly's Directory, 1889)*.

Mr Gulson clearly found that standards in the school had improved by the time of his visit in 1867. He recorded that the children had passed a fair examination, more especially the boys. On the other hand, improvements were still desirable. He suggested that the floors of the schoolroom should be boarded, and that children under 4 years of age should not be attending the school *(MH/12/1280)*.

By 1872, subjects being taught in the school, and examined regularly by the school inspectors, included: religious knowledge; reading; spelling; penman-ship; arithmetic; geography; industrial skills - sewing and knitting for girls, gardening for boys. *(MH/12/1281)*

Every effort was made to give the children a basic education and it was deemed desirable that no child should be allowed to go out to service under 12 years of age.

The end of the workhouse school came with the establishment of local schools in the town, directions from the Local Government Board, and the desire to save costs at the workhouse. In July, 1895 workhouse children were sent out to the local Board schools *(MH/12/1293)*. As it was some distance for them to return mid-day to the workhouse for dinner, the Guardians decided to let the children have pasties from the house to eat at the schools. So, from January, 1896 children took their pasties to school, prepared according to an approved formula:

Pasty recipe	4oz	flour
	0.5oz	lard or dripping
	3oz	meat without bone
	4oz	potatoes
	0.5oz	onions

Source: MH/12/1294

Another change, prompted by the children going to outside schools, was the cessation of the distinctive workhouse clothes being worn, to minimise ridicule by other children. Less conspicuous clothes, even although they never completely disguised that they were workhouse children, replaced the corduroys and other fustian garb of previous years.

In addition to attending the Board schools during the day, all children were still expected to attend the workhouse school at the beginning and end of each day, for industrial training. This comprised instruction in homework, needlework, and house cleaning. In November, 1895 an Inspector's report notes that each child still received 1.75 hours of instruction each day in the workhouse *(MH/12/1293)*. Instruction was given between specified hours:
7.00 - 7.30 am, 5.30 - 6.00 pm, 6.45 - 7.30 pm

As Preston Thomas reflects the closure of the workhouse schools was a great improvement for pauper children. Previously they may never have gone outside the confines of the workhouse, apart from Sundays to go to church. They grew up exclusively in pauper surroundings, and were either cramped by too much discipline, or influenced undesirably by associating with depraved adult inmates. Going to outside schools exposed them to fresh influences. His observations were that "...they tend to make plenty of school friends, and are generally liked by teachers, partly because they are far cleaner than other children (despite the problems noted earlier about adequate washing facilities in the workhouse!), and partly because their attendance is invariably regular..." *(Preston-Thomas, H.)*.

The Infirmary

Conditions in the main house of the workhouse have been described previously as austere, in the infirmary they were worse and very different from our present day picture of a hospital or infirmary. As Inspector Preston Thomas noted "...In 1896 there was not a single workhouse infirmary in the south west on modern lines (for that time)..." *(Preston-Thomas, H.)*. In the case of Bodmin workhouse, contrary to his further observation that in the period to 1908 there was a widespread modernisation or building of new infirmaries, things did not appear to change very much. His successor, Mr E D Court, issued a very critical report to the Guardians in 1912 recommending, amongst other things, that there was a "...need to bring the infirmary more in line with up to date institutions as regards nursing staff and equipment..." *(CG 23 Feb., 1912)*.

The main infirmary building was erected as an integral part of the original workhouse in 1842. There is a record in January 1844 that an unspecified person, Ann Crispin, was to be paid at the rate of £10 per year for assisting in the infirmary *(PU/BOD/1)*. Thereafter, records such as they exist give no indication of any nursing staff being employed until 1870, when the first paid nurse is recorded in the central staffing register for the Bodmin Union *(MH/9/3)*. The normal arrangement during this first 30 years was that "nursing care" in the workhouse infirmary was carried out by the inmates themselves, under the supervision of the Matron.

The first reference to the infirmary is in the report by Inspector Lougley in March 1869 *(MH/12/1280)*. He noted that it had a total of 7 wards and 35 beds. It had been overcrowded during that winter, and he considered that it should be enlarged. His suggestion was that this would be best done by converting the two fever wards into ordinary wards, and erecting two new isolated wards for infectious cases. The fever wards at that time were also being used for other purposes, and inmates with infectious diseases were mixing with ordinary sick cases. This matter was eventually resolved in 1874 when a new isolation block was completed at the top of the recently enlarged workhouse garden *(MH/12/1281)*.

The next matter which concerned Inspectors to Bodmin was the lack of hot water laid on to the infirmary. One of the most critical reports on conditions in the infirmary was issued by Inspector Andrew Fuller when he visited on 30 December 1897 *(MH/12/1295)*. He pointed out the need for "...better sick ward accommodation. The sick wards are very dusty, and the bedsteads appear not to have been dusted for months. The rush matting on bedsteads is in some cases unwholesome, dirty, and dusty. The WC's are not sanitary, and there are no baths or hot water supply to the infirmary. Pauper ward attendants were still being employed in contravention of the General Order issued in August of that year banning them...". Both the Medical Officer and the nurse were also criticised for the poor standards of administration in the sick wards.

By August 1898 the Clerk to the Union Board had confirmed to the Local Government Board that a contract had been entered into for the provision of a bath and a proper hot water boiler in the infirmary. Inspector Preston Thomas confirmed that this work had indeed been carried out when he visited in May 1899. He notes in his report "...am glad to observe that improvement has been made as regards the provision of hot water and a bathroom in the infirmary. I trust that they will be properly utilised..."! *(MH/12/1295)*.

The wards in the infirmary were divided between men and women, but did not cater specifically for the children who were kept in the same wards as the adults. There was concern expressed over this arrangement following the deaths of 4 children in 1909 *(CG 26 Feb., 1909)*. The Board's own Medical Officer wrote to the Guardians pointing out that the hospital was crowded with the old and infirm who needed constant attention. He recommended that the hospital should be enlarged and re-organised, with a children's ward being provided. This recommendation was supported by Inspector Court when he visited in March 1909 *(CG 12 March, 1909)*. He found the women's ward in the infirmary quite full, and, as well as supporting a separate ward for the children, he suggested that the numbers in the infirmary justified the appointment of a night nurse.

Whether or not these recommendations were carried out is not clear from the available records. However, some improvements must have been effected, particularly after Inspector Court's critical report in February 1912 on the lack of staff and equipment in the infirmary. An assistant nurse, as well as a head nurse, appears in the staff register from April 1912 onwards, and on his next visit in September 1912 Mr Court confirmed that "...the infirmary was in good order and the nursing satisfactory...". His only criticism was that the inmates in the infirmary were only getting baths once a fortnight, as there was insufficient hot water for once a week *(CG 20 Sept., 1912)*.

As time had progressed the workhouse infirmary had slowly improved in its standards, and in the nature of its care, largely at the cajoling of Guardians by various Inspectors. The fever outbreaks in the 1800s had ceased; the children had been removed from the workhouse shortly after the beginning of the Great War; and by the end of the 1920s the infirmary was catering increasingly for old people, unable to secure care outside and having to end their days in the workhouse. The local newspaper report on 17 January 1929 refers to the Board's House Committee recommending the appointment of a night nurse due to the increased numbers in the infirmary. Whilst the average number of patients used to be 21-23, it had risen to 30, and with patients having to be attended to at night, the work had become too much for the 2 nurses already employed in the infirmary *(CG 17 Jan., 1929)*.

The Casual Wards

If the main house were austere, and the workhouse infirmary out of date, the casual wards were even more basic. The casual visitors were the most despised for their scrounging habits, and accordingly the least attention was given to their accommodation and conditions. Even by 1924 their wards had not been lit at night, and at that time one of the Guardians admitted on an inspection that "...many bullocks had better places to sleep than had the tramps..." *(CG 3 Oct., 1924)*.

Whilst the numbers of casuals throughout the 1800s were low, it appears that little attempt was made to comply with the regulations appropriate to their treatment at the workhouse. Inspector Preston Thomas noted on his visit in April 1897 that the casuals were not detained overnight, nor bathed on entry (to prevent the spread of infectious diseases), nor made to perform a task. He found the tramps' blankets very damp, but "...got a promise of a better arrangement..."! *(MH/12/1295)*

These lax practices soon changed as the century turned, and, during the period until the outbreak of the Great War, the numbers of casuals calling began to escalate significantly.

In the first place, they were made to perform a task, and detained at the workhouse for 1 night. Initially, it was breaking stones, and sawing wood. In November 1903 10 yards of stone and 1 ton of oak poles was procured in order to put the tramps to work when they arrived at the workhouse *(CG 13 Nov., 1903)*. Police Sergeant Samuel Landrey was appointed as the Assistant Relieving Officer for Vagrants to ensure that there was no disturbance to law and order by casuals, and that the regulations were followed. For his services he was paid the sum of £2 2s/year *(MH/9/3)*.

In 1904 a Special Sub Committee for Vagrants was appointed by the Board and recommended specific tasks for casuals. Stone had been difficult to obtain, but wood was more easily available. The Sub Committee therefore recommended that in future all able bodied tramps should saw 5cwt of oak poles into 8" lengths, or split 240lbs of wood, or bundle 580lbs of wood per day. For this the Union would make a handsome profit, having obtained the wood at 12s per ton delivered, and able to sell it to a Bodmin merchant when bundled for 28s per cwt. *(CG 28 Oct., 1904)*.

By 1909, with numbers of casuals even higher, the problem had become one of finding adequate work for them to do. Wood and stone supplies had become more difficult, and the only possible work at that time was working the corn mill to grind corn, oakum picking to make mats, or digging the trenches for a new drainage scheme to the isolation wards *(CG 3 Dec., 1909)*.

Accommodation for the casuals was in the original fever wards at the front of the workhouse infirmary. There were complaints that these were unheated and damp. At night the doors were locked, and in the winter particularly, unless tramps had their own candles, the nights were long and dark with no lighting provided. In 1912 Inspector Court included the tramp wards in his critical report on the workhouse. He advised that they were unsatisfactory, requiring improvements in ventilation, heating, and water supply. A new set of hammocks, or other substitutes for bedsteads, were also required. Perhaps most unfortunately the regulation that tramps had to be bathed on entry to limit the spread of disease was still not being followed *(CG 23 Feb., 1912)*.

In addition to posing problems at the workhouse, mainly due to their high numbers, tramps were becoming a menace to the population at large *(CG 25 Feb., 1910)*. They were a serious threat to people in lonely parts of the area, and in Bodmin town complaints were made about them frequenting the reading room of the Free Library during the whole afternoon and evening until they could obtain entry to the casual ward at the workhouse *(CG 18 Nov., 1910)*. Begging for food, after leaving the workhouse, was another nuisance to the general population. In an effort to reduce it, a way ticket system had been introduced by some Unions, including Bodmin Union *(CG 13 June, 1913)*. It was a system whereby tickets issued to tramps on leaving the workhouse in the morning could be exchanged for a mid day meal at certain specified relief stations along the way. One of the problems with the scheme was that not all Unions operated it so that its effectiveness was reduced when casuals could not obtain tickets. Other problems were associated with tramps not accepting tickets, or tearing them up after leaving the workhouse because they preferred to beg. Begging was strictly illegal but punishment depended on being caught. In 1913 the Bodmin Union, whilst feeling that this problem was exacerbated by the public being too generous to tramps, and magistrates not punishing them severely enough when they were caught, agreed to support a proposal put forward at a County Conference on the subject, that the way ticket scheme be implemented uniformly across Cornwall by a County Committee of Unions representatives *(CG 5 Sept., 1913)*.

As far as food was concerned, the casual did not share the normal workhouse fare, but was restricted to a far more meagre diet. There are no specific details available for Bodmin Union, but it was probably similar to the majority of Unions where a bread and water diet for casuals was the norm - 8oz dry bread washed down by a draught of cold water for breakfast and supper; 8oz bread, 1½ oz cheese, and a draught of cold water for dinner; a total of 1½ lbs of bread and 1½ oz of cheese for the day *(CG 8 Jan., 1915)*.

On account of the tramps attempting to enlist for the war in 1914 being found to be in such a poor physical condition, the Local Government Board issued revised dietary scales for casuals after the outbreak of war. There is a report in the local newspaper on 2 October 1914 of the new dietary order for tramps being reported to the Bodmin Union Board. It was supposed to include for breakfast and supper, 8oz bread, 1oz margarine or dripping, 1 pt cocoa or broth or gruel; and for dinner, 8oz bread, 2oz cheese, 4oz potatoes. For dinner if travelling between workhouses casuals were usually given either an allowance of bread and cheese for mid day, or a way ticket for a mid day meal at a specified shop of 8oz bread and 2oz cheese (CG 8 Jan., 1915).

During the Great War the numbers of casuals declined drastically almost everywhere, and at Bodmin workhouse the casual wards were practically closed (CG 8 June, 1917). However, by the early 1920s it was necessary to open them again as numbers began to rise. Bodmin Union Board acted more swiftly than other Cornish Boards and became the only one in the County immediately after the war to re-organise a work scheme for casuals. The Board's Vagrancy Committee recommended in March 1924 that no straw mattresses should be provided but that tramps should be left to sleep on the present bare boards; as far as tasks were concerned, these should include wood cutting, 8cwt per day in 10" lengths, and stone breaking,10cwt through a 2" screen (CG 7 March, 1924). These actions by the Bodmin Union Board proved successful as numbers reduced quickly and significantly. The reputation of the hard beds in particular in the casual wards deterred many casuals from visiting Bodmin when they could get a much more comfortable one in the other Cornish workhouses (CG 18 April, 1924).

By the mid 1920s it was felt that limited improvements could be made to the casual wards, without the risk of numbers escalating again. It was agreed to light the wards at night, and to make hot water available, with another steam pipe being provided for more warmth and clothes drying (CG 19 Sept., 1924). The Vagrancy Committee in June 1925 recommended that the Master make enquiries as to disinfecting apparatus, and the provision of night attire for tramps. At that time the tasks required of tramps were the breaking of 7cwt of stone, the cutting of 8cwt of wood, or digging, pumping, or grinding of corn, all over an 8 hour day. The Ministry of Health Inspector called attention to the remaining inadequate accommodation for women tramps, including no bath, disinfecting chamber, or night clothes (CG 12 June, 1925). Women casuals were required to be employed by the Matron in washing or scrubbing. By September it was agreed to purchase 12 nightshirts for casuals at a cost of 6s 6d each, and to invite tenders for a bathroom and disinfecting chamber for the women's casual ward (CG 4 Sept., 1925).

The success of all these measures to be reasonable to the needs of casuals, as well as deterring them, met a setback when the Casual Vagrancy Order 1925 came into effect. It required that all tasks had in future to be measured by time, rather than by quantity. Immediately, casuals saw an opportunity to work less, and the Master reported that instead of chopping 8cwts of wood per day, only 1½ cwt was being achieved since the Order *(CG 8 Jan., 1926)*. The Board made representations to the Ministry of Health, but to no effect, to have the Order amended, and made more discretionary. The Board was advised that tramps should be given 8 hours work, and if they did not do a reasonable amount in that time they should be taken before a Magistrate, charged accordingly *(CG 2 April, 1926)*. Unfortunately, success with the Magistrates was limited and they were not as supportive as desired by the Board. The Master reported a case in January 1927 where the task given to a tramp was to scrub the bed boards on which tramps had slept, and to wash the floor. He had taken half the day to scrub the beds rather than 2 hours, and, after dinner, when told by the Porter to wash the floor, he had absolutely refused to do so. When taken to the Magistrate, he had only been given 1 day's imprisonment, which effectively meant an immediate discharge *(CG 7 Jan., 1927)*.

Problems with getting the casuals to perform their tasks continued right to the end and the demise of the Board. In February 1930 the local newspaper reported that 6 tramps had been brought before Magistrates for refusing to do their allotted tasks at the workhouse. All pleaded guilty and were sent off for 14 days hard labour on this occasion, despite their pleas in mitigation that there was no heat in the casual ward and, having only 3 blankets to share, they were too cold to work *(CG 20 Feb., 1930)*.

Ironically, it was the casuals who were the last occupants of the workhouse, with conditions being considerably improved for them compared to earlier times. As the last resident inmates were transferred elsewhere in the County, renovations in 1936 provided new quarters and some 47 beds for casuals *(Kelly's Directory for Cornwall, 1939)*. With central heating, electric light, baths, plenty of washing facilities, and special apparatus for fumigating clothes, Members of the East Central Guardians Committee described the quarters as a new hotel *(CG 7 May, 1936)*, and they must indeed have seemed palatial compared to the conditions which casuals had endured for the previous 94 years.

Plate 14: Dr Nat Coulson
(CG 16 Feb., 1906)

Plate 15: Mr Richard Elford
(CG 18 June, 1926)

Plate 16: Mr John Pethybridge
(CG 27 May, 1927)

Chapter 8

Recollections

"Bodmin Union Institution - How the Inmates Live...A Pen Picture" is an article which appears in the local newspaper, the Cornish Guardian on 17 December 1926. Communicated probably by a former inmate it gives an impression of life in the workhouse during the 1920s.

The Institution at Bodmin is commodious, scrupulously clean, and distinctly hygienic in every way. Mr Henry F Benny is the competent head of the establishment and his efforts for the welfare and comfort of those under his supervision are ably seconded by the Matron (Mrs H F Benny) and other officers, whose popularity, created by their untiring anxiety for the well being of those under their care, is as genuine as it is general. Indeed, it is no hyperbole to assert that no Institution could have a more capable, sympathetic set of officials, whose services, it need hardly be added, are highly appreciated by the Guardians and inmates alike.

The inmates are well looked after and there is wholesome food. The main problem is the work they are required to do, and the fact that it is nothing more than mere exercise.

What hurts the bulk of the inmates is their confinement. True they are allowed certain liberty and their friends and relatives are allowed to visit them weekly, yet the privilege of freedom is curtailed and this rankles in most of them.

Even some of the old men, particularly during the summer months, take their discharges periodically to taste freedom, but after a while they return again.

On the other hand there are some inmates who very rarely, if ever, go outside and this breeds a very uneven, cantankerous temperament. As often as not they are ostracised by their former chums.

The effects produced by the workhouse environment cannot honestly be said to be conducive to good health, particularly in the winter months when the inmates are prevented from rambling in the grounds and taking the fresh air which has such a stimulating influence. The penned up process is distinctly detrimental to well being. It generates melancholia, as well as irritability and temper. Continually one sees faces which suggest fretfulness, despondency, and a sullen revolt against life and circumstances.

The majority of men lead an empty, uneventful life, and although the soul degrading restrictions and humiliations of the bad old days are practically evils of the past (the Poor Law system having greatly changed for the better since

Dickens wrote of "Bumbledom") there is still room for improvement with regard to liberty, the innovation of useful work for the inmates, and reading facilities. Under the circumstances however the general body of inmates ought to be thankful that such an Institution is in existence.

Notwithstanding the fact that the Poor Law is an admirable one, there are several distressing features about it. For instance, when a man leaves a Union Institution, irrespective of the time he might have been there, he is in exactly the same predicament as he was when he entered the House - broke financially, still without a situation, and in the generality of cases, shabbily attired. To turn a man adrift without money, in poor clothes, and with no employment to go to, certainly retards rather than facilities his restart in life.

* * * * *

Perhaps the most famous inmate of the Bodmin Union workhouse was Dr Nat Coulson. Born in Penzance in 1853 he and his mother fell on hard times and he was taken into the workhouse at Bodmin in 1860, aged 7years old. Here he remained for 4 years before being placed by the Guardians with a Mr Thomas Hore at Penquite Farm, near Lostwithiel. In 1869 at the age of 16 he left Penquite and enlisted in the Royal Navy as a boy entrant. However, life at sea did not agree with his health and after purchasing his freedom in 1874, he took a ship to Pennsylvania and got a job as a clerk. After a short stay he went to New Zealand for 12 months, before returning to San Francisco in 1877. He entered the university there in 1880 and after studying for 5 years left with a degree as a Doctor of Dental Surgery. Once qualified he set up a most successful dental practice and quickly became the most famous dentist in San Francisco. He became a household name with the residents of the city *(CG 16 Feb., 1906)*.

Despite his success he never forgot his origins back in Bodmin and Lostwithiel. In 1901 he paid a return visit which is reported in the Cornish Guardian newspaper on 16 February 1902:

He consequently came to Lostwithiel, and revisited the scenes of his early life. One of the first places to which he went after seeing his friends at Penquite Farm was to the scene of his childhood's shelter at Bodmin Union workhouse, where he made himself known, and interested himself in all its work and surroundings. Although risen in the world he was not ashamed to inform the inmates that he was himself at one time an inmate of their institution like themselves, and he evidently felt a pride in relating to the children his early life under the workhouse roof. He also remembered that an act of kindness when he was one of them was valued much more than anyone placed in more fortunate circumstances can have any idea of, and now he was able to do so he cheerfully did what he could to give the inmates a happy day."

The paper reported separately that Dr Coulson had sent 10s to the workhouse towards the end of 1901 as a contribution to the inmates' Christmas treat *(CG 2 Nov., 1901)*.

In 1907 Dr Coulson deposited a sum of money with the editor of the local Cornish Guardian newspaper to assist Bodmin boys wishing to emigrate to America. The arrangement was that each emigrant repaid his loan of this money as soon as possible to enable the next one to follow. The fund was still in use in 1913 *(CG 8 May, 1968)*.

Whilst enjoying the success of his life Dr Coulson always wanted to repay the kindnesses which he had experienced whilst in Lostwithiel as a child. When the Mayor of Lostwithiel commenced an appeal for the provision of a chain of office for use by Mayors of the Borough, Nat Coulson gave a donation sufficient to cover 9 links in it which are in memory of the 9 earliest Mayors of the Borough. On another occasion he gave £100 to the town to complete the people's park which was being laid out at the beginning of the century *(CG 16 Feb., 1906)*.

* * * * *

The reluctance of Casuals to work and their will to buck the system is recalled in an interview with a tramp which the Cornish Guardian reported on 1 September 1911. It is entitled "A Tramps Story - Workshy relates his experiences". This particular individual was known to the tramping fraternity from Land' End to John O'Groats as the "gentleman" tramp, by reason of his clean and tidy appearance. By his craftiness he recalls how he managed to find a comfortable subsistence, as well as solving the problem of how to beg without being caught.

I belong to the noble society of the NWBM (no work between meals). I have had a decent education and was a corporal when discharged from the Grenadier Guards at the end of the Boer War. I've come down to Cornwall and here I stop. I don't cross the Tamar but beg my way all through the County and back again. I find the Cornish people are very good and the better you are known, and the oftener you call on 'em, the better they like you...A man must keep himself respectable if he wants to get on in this tramping line. Tell them a good yarn and they won't say no when you ask them for something...

I was begging in the main street in Bodmin one day when a policeman came round the corner just as the lady was bringing out some cake. I told the woman to go back with the cake, and just as the policeman got within hearing distance, I said "I am sorry I cannot persuade you to join our company madam". The policeman thought I was an insurance agent or something, and passed on. I begged all through the street, and when I got to the top I counted up in coppers 2s 9d.

I have never been "had" for begging, though I sometimes go through a whole street begging until I am satisfied...No! You can't go into the workhouse if you've got any money, but you can leave it outside..."

* * * * *

In 1927 Mr John Pethybridge retired after spending 30 years serving the Bodmin Board of Guardians as their Clerk. On 27 May 1927 the Cornish Guardian reports that after tea in the Board room at the workhouse he was presented with a watercolour of Roughtor in the House Committee room. In responding to the Chairman's appreciation of his long service Mr Pethybridge recalled some of the most significant issues during his time:

...Time has brought its changes. There were only three members of the Board now who were there when he was elected. Of course, many who were then members were living still, but he was happy to think there were some still associated with them who were there when he first began. He referred to Mr Phillips, Mr Trevail, and Mr W E Menhenick as being members when he was first appointed and said it was very nice to have met some of the old members that day. Speaking of some of the old stalwarts who had gone he mentioned the late Mr Edward Pollard who was such a great man on the Assessment Committee in those early days; the late Mr Tom Baron (father of the present chairman) who was such an economist; and their dear old friend the late Mr R K Elford who did so much for the internal affairs of the House. Then there was Colonel Alms and ladies like Mrs Foster, Mrs Paul, and Miss Guy. He could not help thinking of some of those who did their work so well in those by gone days and was glad to know some were still alive. There was Mrs Honey, for instance, who did a great work on the Board. He congratulated the Board on having such a strong force of lady members. Some Boards had not a single lady member which was to be regretted. He always had the highest respect for their work. In many respects the lot of the inmates had benefited enormously by the good work of the ladies as had the children before and since their removal to the Scattered Homes.

There had not been very serious changes in regard to the administrative side of the Board. They would remember perhaps the time when the question of putting the children in the Scattered Homes was a burning one, but he thought they were all satisfied that the result had been satisfactory. He also remembered the abolition of the pay stations (for out relief), which was another reform which had turned out satisfactorily and to the advantage of all concerned. Then the introduction of the Old Age Pensions Act had tended to *relieve the numbers of those in receipt of out relief. Many improvements too had been effected to the infirmary which used to be looked upon as a last resort and people were afraid to go there. But now with the developments which had been effected their infirmary was a home of rest under the direction of their medical officer and nursing staff, for the sick of the neighbourhood...*

* * * * *

One of the most respected members of the Bodmin Union Board was a Mr R K Elford. He represented St Tudy parish for a great many years and his background, which perhaps also gives a feel for the way in which the Board as a whole carried out its duties, is recounted in the report of his death, one week after his 90th birthday, in the Cornish Guardian newspaper on 18 June 1926.

He had been born at St Cleer in June 1836 and after moving to St Tudy at the age of 17 lived for the rest of his life at Penvose. From an early age he took an interest in religious matters. He identified with the United Methodist denomination and was the superintendent of the St Tudy Sunday School for a long time. He was also a keen supporter of the British Foreign Bible Society, as well as supporting other religious denominations.

Mr Elford was known over a wide area for his generosity, and various charitable organisations benefited from his financial support. He was also a member of the East Cornwall Hospital management committee.

It was early in his life that Mr Elford began an interest in public work. For a great many years he represented St Tudy on the old Trigg Highway Board, which later merged into the Bodmin Rural District Council. He was one of the first County Councillors, a member of the Mental Hospital Visiting Committee, and a County Magistrate.

It was however in connection with the Poor Law side of his work that he was so well known and his services so much esteemed. His kindly and generous disposition and cheery word made him a great favourite among the inmates of the Bodmin Poor Law Institution and his periodical visits were eagerly looked forward to. For many years he held the position of chairman of the House Committee of the Bodmin Board of Guardians, of which authority he became to be affectionately known as "The Father of the Board" - a portrait of him under this title occupied a place of honour on the wall of the Board room in the workhouse. When declining years prevented his active involvement he was co-opted to the Board. He retired at the last triennial elections but was sent a special invitation to attend meetings of the Board whenever he felt able to do so (CG 18 June, 1926).

* * * * *

Herbert Preston Thomas was one of the Local Government Board Inspectors, responsible for visiting workhouses and ensuring that they and the Guardians responsible for them were following the Government regulations. He took charge of the South West district, Devon and Cornwall, towards the end of 1896 and retired in 1908. In 1909 he published his memoirs which give an insight into "The work and play of a Government Inspector".

On his appointment to the South West in 1896 he records finding the workhouses in the district to be inferior to those in the eastern counties, from where he had moved. The arrangements for bathing and washing were often deficient. The sick were generally lodged in old fashioned and ill ventilated wards without the appliances that modern practice of the day required. The children were confined too much in a pauper atmosphere. Imbeciles were often a nuisance to the sane.

Bodmin was included on his itinerary of visits, and on his farewell visit to the Bodmin Union Board in 1908 he told the Guardians that "...he thought the workhouse was somewhat old fashioned, with cold comfort in the nursery which still had a stone floor..." *(CG 13 March, 1908)*.

In his published recollections he makes no specific reference to Bodmin, but records his general impressions on what he found when visiting throughout Devon and Cornwall. Bodmin was no doubt similar to the average that he visited. The main thing which struck him about the inmates was their contentedness. He found that "...in 9 out of 10 rural workhouses, the general disposition of inmates was to be grateful, rather than to growl or be discontented...the quiet content of the country contrasts with the seething turbulence of the town workhouses..." *(Preston -Thomas, H.)*.

The worst class in the workhouse according to Preston Thomas was the mothers of illegitimate children. Outside the workhouse they were apt to fall prey to drink and be unable to support themselves. Within the workhouse they were sometimes liable to give trouble.

On the other hand, he found that the old men usually seemed cheerful, especially when given something to do by the Master which suited them. The more occupation they had, the less they were inclined to grumble.

His observations on the inmates agree with the comments reported some years later in 1923 by one of the Guardians, a Mr R Roose. He reported to the Union Board in his capacity as a workhouse visitor. He found that everything was in good order and that the inmates were contented and comfortable. One old man who was sitting by a big fire said to him "Maister, we don't want anything better than we have got here", and another added "Yes, and baccy to smoke" *(CG 9 March, 1923)*.

Chapter 9

The Ending and a New Beginning

On Saturday 23 March 1930 the Bodmin Board of Guardians met in the Board room at the workhouse for the last time. The Government had enacted the Local Government Act 1929 which meant that on 1 April 1930 their powers passed to the Cornwall County Council, and the Union Board passed into history. To mark the end of an era arrangements were made for a group photograph of Board members in the grounds of Berry Tower House, as they still referred to it, and later, on the day of their final meeting, they dined together at the Royal Hotel in Bodmin *(CG 13 March,1930)*. The Guardians marked the occasion with a mixture of celebration and regret. Celebration for the loyal service rendered by successive Guardians over the past 93 years, who did their best to care for the poor of the Bodmin area; and regret that the changes would mean a loss of the personal touch, local knowledge and local popular control with bureaucracy by officials.

As far as the Cornwall County Council was concerned, it received the functions, properties, and staff of all the Union Boards in the County. The Public Assistance Committee, with its 39 members representing all the Union areas in the County, was to be the new central body at Truro, responsible for administering the provisions for the poor in the 1929 Act. Cornwall was divided into 5 areas for poor relief work, with day to day responsibilities devolved to a new Committee for each area *(CG 8 Aug., 1929)*. Bodmin Union was combined with the Unions of Liskeard and St Germans to form the East Cornwall Guardians Committee. Initially, the meetings of the new Committee were rotated between the workhouses at Liskeard, Bodmin, and Torpoint *(CG 27 March, 1930)*. However, as with most reorganisations, rationalisation and further change was soon on the agenda. After just over 12 months it was resolved to hold all future meetings of the Committee at Liskeard, and not to rotate to the other places. An assessment was made of all institutions and children's homes in the County. Arising out of this exercise was a recommendation to close the institutions at Bodmin, Camelford, Truro, and St Columb as soon as possible for poor law purposes. Bodmin, Truro, and St Columb were to be offered to the Mental Deficiency Committee as institutions for the reception of mental defectives *(CG 6 Aug.,1931)*. By the end of 1936 the local newspaper reports indicate that the Bodmin Institution finally closed, as far as continuing to accommodate long stay inmates *(CG 17 Dec., 1936)*.

BODMIN BOARD'S FAREWELL.

[Sandy, Truro.

Back Row:—Messrs. W. H. Hocking, A. H. Runnalls, J. E. Marshall, W. Keat, G. Riddle, J. Jeffery (Relieving Officer), H. E. Bastard, J. F. Wills, J. H. Hawken, E. T. Hawkey, S. T. Button, A. W. Downing, N. Cleave, R. J. Knight, W. Cole, W. H. Sandry, D. Strout, T. Harris (Relieving Officer).

Middle Row:—Messrs. J. G. Harris, J. B. Tucker, G. J. Strout, S. M. Dustow, J. M. Edwards, N. Mutton, F. H. Andrew, T. Baron, E. J. Burton, G. C. Carpenter, Nurse Heyward, Mr. T. H. Dyer, Miss Best (Matron's Assistant), Miss Jones (Mental Attendant), Rev. C. F. Jones, Commander Edgcumbe, Messrs. W. Symons, T. D. Runnals, J. Stephens, H. B. Laity, W. Crago, W. S. Chapman, W. Richards, E. Hill (Porter), M. P. Menhinick, W. A. Williams (Press Representative).

Front Row:—Messrs. T. Warne, W. J. Brown, H. Eddy, Mrs. D. M. Pease, Mrs. H. M. Williams, Mrs. A. Brewer, Messrs. W. Phillips, E. W. Gill (Clerk), E. G. Martyn (Chairman), J. H. Trevail (Vice-Chairman), C. T. Trevail, Mrs. T. H. Spear, Mrs. G. S. Bricknell, Mrs. W. J. Adams, Mrs. Benney (Matron), Mr. H. F. Benny (Master), Mrs. Hill (Industrial Trainer).

During the previous year several of the inmates were transferred, according to their wishes, to the institutions at either St Austell or Liskeard, whichever one was nearer to their relatives (CG 1 Aug., 1935). On the other hand, it appears that casuals continued to be given shelter at Bodmin and the local newspaper reports that renovations were carried out to provide new quarters for casuals at Berry Tower House (CG 7 May, 1936). Kelly's Directory for Cornwall of 1939 contains the entry for the Bodmin workhouse of casual wards, with accommodation comprising 47 beds, under the supervision of a Mr W B Hughes as superintendent, and Mrs N M Hughes as matron. With the onset of the Second World War the workhouse era at Bodmin had truly passed.

The main infirmary building, with the exception of the original detached fever wards later to become the casual wards, was the first to be privately acquired for subdivision into residential use. The original workhouse garden, behind the former infirmary building, was developed as St Dominic's Close, a small residential estate of some 8 bungalows. The workhouse garden at the side of the buildings was subdivided into private plots and sold for individual bungalows to be erected. The isolation wards built in this garden area were used for some time in connection with the county constabulary for storage purposes. Today they are in private hands, and the building has been renovated.

After closure, the main problem for the County Council was what to do with the workhouse buildings - the front entrance block, the central block with its attached kitchen building, and the casual ward buildings. For almost 50 years, from the late 1930s to the late 1980s, they laid either vacant or in partial use, slowly deteriorating. Small businesses, including a dairy, furniture storage, an electrical business and a carpentry workshop used the buildings during this period.

In July 1987, as a national property boom swept the country, the County Council seized its chance to dispose of them. The whole complex was auctioned with planning permission for conversion into 1- and 2-bedroomed residential flats. A new beginning for the old workhouse was conceived with an innovative conversion scheme. Purchased by a firm of developers based in Cumbria, Haven Homes (South West) Ltd., building works were carried out quickly during 1988-1990, creating a total of 35 flats with parking and landscaping. After completion of the scheme, with the property boom over, the developers went into receivership, leaving the owners of the new properties to form their own residents association to manage the development. The Bodmin Union Workhouse, subsequently Berry Tower House and Institution, continues, some 160 years after it was originally built, as Castle Hill Court, the new name given to it after this latest conversion.

Appendix 1:

Occupants of the Bodmin Union Workhouse Recorded on Census Night 3 April, 1881

OFFICIALS

Name	Age	Position
WHALE, Tom	32	Master
WHALE, Mary Elizabeth	31	Matron
WHALE, Banfield Hawke	2	Son
MITCHELL, John	64	Porter
DAVEY, William Thomas	23	Schoolmaster
SMITH, Marcia	45	Ind. Trainer
TUCKER, Elizabeth	64	Nurse

INMATES

Name	Age	Name	Age
ADAMS, Bathsheba	69	KEAT, Susan	22
ALLEN, Raleigh	12	KEAT, Millicent	3
BATE, Elizabeth	10	KELLOW,Jane	78
BATE, Thomas	9	KELLY,Thomas	11
BAWDEN, John	83	KELLY, Charles	9
BECKHAM,John	20	KENNEDY,George	19
BENNETT, John	53	KNIGHT, Ann	50
BLAKE, Emma	12	LAWRY, James	27
BLAKE, Emma	10	LAWRY, Tabitha	44
BLAKE, Susan	8	MARK,William P	12
BOWDEN, George	65	MARK, Edith	7
BRAY, John	61	MARKS, Philip	75
BREWER, Louisa	1	MASTERS, Mary Ann	33
BROWN, Sarah	36	MASTERS, Harriet	1
BROWN, Sarah Jane	12	MASTERS, Susan	20
BROWN, Louisa	8	MASTERS, Anna Maria	2
BROWN, James	1	MASTERS, William James	3m
BROWN, William	72	MAY, Henry	9
BUNNY, Thomas	72	MAY, Edith	6
BUNT, Mary	86	MILLET, Isaac	70
BUSCOMBE, Ann	76	MULLIS, Robert	10

Name	Age	Name	Age
CALLAWAY, Lois	18	PEARCE, John	11
CALLAWAY, William L	1m	PEARCE, Theodre	69
CHAMPION, Martha	26	PHILLIPS, Ann	40
CHAMPION, Ethel Martha	2	PHILLIPS, John	7
CHAMPION, William George	7m	PHILLIPS, Millicent	6
COCK, William	73	PHILLIPS, William T	3
COUCH, John Henry	12	PHILLIPS, Henry	1
COUCH, Charles	9	PHILLIPS, Thomas	4
COURTS, Louisa	47	POLKINGHORNE, Rebecca	20
COWLING, Joseph	83	POLKINGHORNE, Albert	10m
CRADDOCK, Temperance	85	POMROY, Stephen	12
DINGLE, Mary	84	RETALLICK, Mary	30
DYER, Clara	19	RETALLICK, Annie	9
EDE, Richard	37	RETALLICK, Bernard	5
EDWARDS, George Exel	11	RETALLICK, Marwood	4
GLANVILLE, Jane	36	RETALLICK, Harriet	29
GLANVILLE, Ernest	6m	RETALLICK, Henry	7
GOULD, William	81	RETALLICK, Archibald	5
GOYEN, Sarah	88	ROSCORL, Sarah	30
GROWDEN, Mathew	81	ROSCORL, Maud	10
HALEY, Jane	77	ROSCORL, George	1
HARRIS, Thomas	12	ROWE, Ann	72
HARRIS, Selina	67	SANDY, David	54
HAWKE, Samuel	40	STEER, Elizabeth	86
HEARD, Sarah	38	THOMAS, Jane	29
HICK, Polly	25	TRELOAR, John	12
HILL, Alfred	56	TRUAN, Jane	60
HOARE, Thomas	13	TRYHALL, William	47
HOARE, Samuel	11	TUCKER, Edward	66
JONES, Susan	27	TUCKER, Susan	60
JONES, Elizabeth Ann	6	VARCOE, John	57
JONES, Annie	1	WARNE, John	66
JOY, Lucy	30	WORDEN, Anna	34
JOY, Edward	7	WORDEN, Emma	6
KEAST, William Henry	20	WORDEN, William John	1

Source: *1881 Census record obtained from microfilm of the original Enumerator's books, Courtney Library, the Royal Institution of Cornwall, Truro*

Appendix 2:

Key Events in the History of The Bodmin Union Workhouse

The Early Years 1834-1870

1834 Poor Law Amendment Act enacted by Parliament;

1837 First meeting of Bodmin Union Board of Guardians with William Hicks elected as Clerk. Agreement to purchase site near Berry Tower for new workhouse;

1838 Advertisements for architect to submit plans and terms for building new workhouse, and for local builders to submit prices to build it;

1838 William and Sarah Truman appointed and in due course become Master and Matron of new workhouse for first 27 years;

1839 Authority given by Poor Law Commissioners for loan sanction to proceed with building new workhouse;

1840 Building work commenced on site;

1842 New workhouse largely completed, with a capacity for 250 inmates, at a total cost of £7375;

1842 Elizabeth Lawry appointed as first schoolmistress of workhouse school;

1847 John Mitchell appointed as first porter at the workhouse;

1847 Critical report by visiting Commissioner on arrangements and standards in workhouse school;

1869 Visiting Poor Law Inspector reported great deal of fever in workhouse;

The Reforming Years 1870-1915

1870 First nurse appointed in workhouse infirmary;

1874 Completion of isolation wards to accommodate infectious cases in a new building separate from the main workhouse infirmary, and built in the recently extended workhouse garden. Old fever ward buildings converted into accommodation for casual callers;

1878 Tom and Mary Whale appointed as Master and Matron for the next 27 years;

1880 Replacement of cesspools for foul drainage by provision of new sewerage system and connection to main town system;

1894	National change in legislation to allow women and working class people to stand for election as local Guardians on the Union Board;
1895	Closure of workhouse school and all children to attend local board schools in the town;
1895	Agreement for continuous supply of mains water by Bodmin Water Company to replace supply from workhouse well;
1899	Provision of hot water and bathroom in workhouse infirmary;
1904	The term "workhouse" removed by the renaming of Bodmin Union Workhouse as Berry Tower House;
1908	Gas lighting installed to replace candles and oil lamps;
1909	Critical report nationally by Royal Commission on the operation of the Poor Law system;
1909	Old age pensions introduced and labour exchanges established nationally to assist those searching for work;
1909	Critical report by visiting inspector on the condition of the children in the workhouse;
1909	Dramatic increase in the number of casual callers at the workhouse;
1911	Unemployment insurance introduced nationally;
1912	Improvements in the staffing and equipment in the workhouse infirmary;
1912	Richard and Mary Benny appointed Master and Matron of the workhouse for the next 11 years;
1913	National Order made relaxing many central controls in favour of greater local discretion by Union Boards. All workhouses in future to be referred to as Institutions;
1913	All girls under 15 years old moved out of the workhouse to live in a new scattered home built off Beacon Road;
1914	Telephone connected to the workhouse;
1915	All boys under 15 years old moved out of the workhouse to live in a house acquired to serve as a scattered home in Berrycombe Hill;

The Concluding Years 1915-1939

1917	Decline in numbers of casual callers due to the effects of the Great War and temporary closure of casual wards;
1919	New Ministry of Health assumed responsibility for Poor Law administration;

1923   Mr & Mrs H F Benny appointed Master and Matron of the workhouse for the final 13 years;

1923   Neville Chamberlain, MP, with his dislike of elected Union Guardians, appointed Minister of Health, 1923, and 1924-29;

1925   Increase in numbers of casual callers again, contained by organised work scheme of labour tasks;

1929   Reorganisation of local government to eliminate local Union Boards and transfer powers to County Councils;

1930   Bodmin Union Board met for final time, after 93 years in existence, and responsibility for Bodmin Institution passed to East Cornwall Guardians Committee of Cornwall County Council;

1936   All long term residents in the former workhouse moved out to other institutions and Bodmin Union workhouse effectively closed for long term care. Renovations carried out to continue providing better standard casual ward accommodation;

1939   Onset of Second World War and the workhouse era in Bodmin finally closes entirely.

A New Beginning

1987   Main workhouse buildings sold at auction by the Cornwall County Council to a development company, Haven Homes (South West) Ltd for conversion into a complex of 35 residential flats;

1990   Conversion scheme completed and the complex re-named Castle Hill Court.

Sources

Barton, R.M. *Life in Cornwall at the end of the Nineteenth Century - Extracts from the West Briton Newspaper 1876-1899.* Bradford Barton, Truro, 1974.

Bennett, A. *Cornwall Through the Mid Nineteenth Century.* Kingfisher Railway Productions, 1987.

Burton, W.J.P. & Stephens, J. *"When We Were* Boys - *and some time after"* Cornish Guardian 19 April, 1928, 26 April, 1928, and 3 May, 1928.

Census records (1851 & 1881). *Courtney Library, the Royal Institution of Cornwall, Truro.*

Census records (1861, 1871 & 1891). *Cornish Studies Library, Redruth.*

CG - *Cornish Guardian newspaper, County Library, Bodmin.*

Checkland, S.G. & Checkland, E.O.A. *The 1834 Poor Law Report.* Penguin, Harmondsworth, 1974.

Collier, W.F. *Tales and Sayings of William Robert Hicks of Bodmin.* Simpkin, Marshall, Hamilton, Kent & Co., Ltd., London, and William Brendon & Son, Plymouth, 1893.

Crowther, M.A. *The Workhouse System 1834-1929 - The History of an English Social Institution.* Batsford Ltd.,1981.

Dickens, A. *The Architect and the Workhouse.* Architectural Review, **160**, 1976.

Englander, D. *Poverty and Poor Law Reform in 19th Century Britain, 1834-1914.* Longman,1998

English Heritage *Bodmin Union Workhouse.* Unpublished Report by R. Taylor, May, 1992.

Harrod's Directory of Cornwall/Devon 1878.

Herber, M.D. (in association with the Society of Genealogists) *Ancestral Trails - The Complete Guide to British Genealogy and Family History.* Stroud:Sutton, 1997.

H M Poor Law Commissioners *First Annual Report of the Poor Law Commissioners for England & Wales, 1835.*

Kelly's Directories of Cornwall 1873, 1888, 1889, 1893, 1914, 1930, 1939.

Local Government Board *Annual Reports 1871-1914*

Long, L.E. *An Old Cornish Town - Bygone Bodmin in Essay and Anecdote.* Bodmin Books Ltd., 1975.

Longmate, N. *The Workhouse: A Social History.* Temple-Smith, 1974.

May, T. *The Victorian Workhouse.* Shire Publications Ltd.,1999

MH/9/3 *Poor Law Union Staff Register, containing details of staff employed in the Bodmin Union.* Public Record Office, Kew.

MH/12/1274-1295 - *Poor Law Union papers relating to the Bodmin Union.* Public Record Office, Kew.

Planning permission records. North Cornwall District Council, Barn Lane, Bodmin.

Poor Law Board *Annual Reports 1849-1870.*

Poor Law Commission *Annual Reports 1835-1848.*

Preston-Thomas, H. *The Work and Play of a Government Inspector.* William Blackwood & Sons, 1909.

PU/BOD/1-11 - *Bodmin Union Minute Books 1842-1916.* County Record Office, Truro.

PU/BOD/39 - *Bodmin Union Officers' Salaries Register 1878-1929.* County Record Office, Truro.

Todd, A. *Basic Sources for Family History; 1.Back to the early 1800's.* Allen & Todd, 1994.